Writing Handbook

GRADE

3

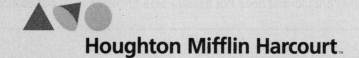

Houghton Mifflin Harcourt.

Contents

Contents

How to Use This Book

Writing is a great tool. It can help you solve problems as well as express yourself. For example, you can use it to nail down an idea or hammer out a point. This handbook will help you discover ways to use this tool well.

What Is a Handbook?

If writing is a tool, then this handbook is the how-to manual. It contains clear definitions, strategies, models, and key practice. Refer to its pages as much as you need to before, during, and after writing.

Sections of This Book

This handbook has three sections:

 Writing Forms—Definitions, labels, and models of key writing forms

 Writing Strategies—Ideas and methods that you can use for every kind of writing

3 **Writing Models and Forms**—Examples of good writing

How to Find Information

Find information in this book in two different ways:

- **Use the contents page.** Find the section you need, and then turn to the entry that most closely matches the topic you want.
- **Use the tabs at the top of left-hand pages.** The names of the tabs change with each section.

Purposes for Writing

Before you write, one of the first things you should think about is your purpose, or reason for writing. There are many purposes for writing, but the main ones are to inform, to explain, to narrate, or to persuade.

● To Inform

To inform is to give information. This means writing and sharing facts and details. Some kinds of writing that inform are reports, informative paragraphs, and instructions.

● To Explain

To explain means to tell about a topic by telling what, why, and how. Some kinds of writing that explain are instructions, how-to paragraphs, and problem-solution paragraphs.

● To Narrate

To narrate means to tell a story with a beginning, middle, and end. Some examples of narrative writing include personal narratives, fictional narratives, and biographies.

● To Persuade

To persuade means to convince someone else to agree with your opinion or take an action. Opinion and persuasive essays and book reviews are kinds of writing that persuade.

Understanding Task, Audience, and Purpose (TAP)

Knowing your purpose is one way to help you start to write. You should also think about your **audience**, or for whom you are writing. For example, the words you use in writing to a friend are likely to be different from those you use with someone you have never met.

Knowing your purpose and your audience will help you select your **task**, or writing form. For example, if you want to tell your classmates about a fun experience you had, you can share the information as a personal narrative or a poem.

Before you start to write, decide your task, audience, and purpose, or **TAP**. Your task is what you are writing. Your audience is for whom you are writing. Your purpose is why you are writing. Your teacher may give you the TAP for an assignment. Sometimes you will choose on your own.

Ask yourself these questions.

Task: <u>What</u> am I writing?

Do I want to write a letter, a report, or something else?

Audience: For <u>whom</u> am I writing?

Am I writing for a teacher, myself, or someone else?

Purpose: <u>Why</u> am I writing?

Am I writing to persuade someone, to give information, or for another reason?

The Writing Process

The writing process is a five-stage strategy that was created to help you write well. It helps you think through what you're going to write and then change it and improve it along the way. Finally, it helps you to make your writing better. The best part about the writing process is that you can go back to any of the stages while you're writing.

The writing process helps you move back and forth between the different stages of your writing.

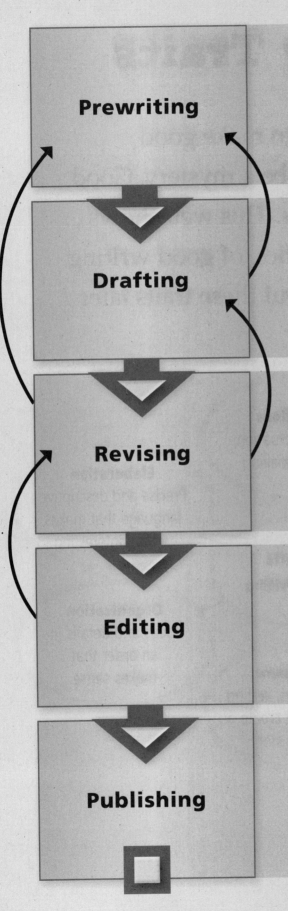

Prewriting

Identify your TAP—task, audience, and purpose. First, choose a topic. Then gather and organize information about the topic.

Drafting

Put your ideas in full sentences. Don't worry about making mistakes now. You can fix them later.

Revising

Read your writing to see how well it matches your purpose. Meet with a partner to talk about how to make your draft better.

Editing

Now is the time to correct any spelling, grammar, usage, mechanics, and capitalization mistakes.

Publishing

Decide how you want to publish your work. Who will you show it to? How will you share it?

The Writing Traits

Knowing what it takes to make good writing doesn't have to be a mystery. Good writing has certain traits. This web shows the traits, or characteristics, of good writing. You will learn more about these traits later in the book.

Conventions
Correct punctuation, grammar, spelling

Evidence
Details and ideas that develop a topic

Elaboration
Precise and descriptive language that makes writing interesting

The Traits of Good Writing

Purpose
A writer's reason for writing

Organization
Ideas and details in an order that makes sense

Development
Vivid characters, setting, and events that create an interesting story

Traits Checklist

Ask yourself these questions as you practice writing.

☑ **Evidence**	Do I explain ideas with details and examples? Do I support opinions with facts and details?
☑ **Organization**	Are my ideas in a clear order? Do I have a beginning, middle, and ending? Do I use transitions, such as time-order words?
☑ **Purpose**	Is my reason for writing clear?
☑ **Elaboration**	Do I use vivid and precise words and phrases to develop my topic or tell a story?
☑ **Development**	Did I include details that help readers visualize the characters and settings? Did I tell the story events in an interesting way?
☑ **Conventions**	Are my spelling, grammar, and punctuation correct?

Descriptive Paragraph

A **descriptive paragraph** tells what something is like. It uses specific words and details to paint a picture of the topic. These words help the reader see, feel, hear, and sometimes smell or taste what is being described.

Parts of a Descriptive Paragraph

- A topic sentence that introduces the main idea
- Exact words and vivid details that tell the reader exactly what the topic is like
- Sensory details that help the reader see, hear, smell, taste, and feel things
- A closing sentence that wraps up the paragraph

pencils

Topic Sentence
Tells the main idea

Exact Words
Paint a clear picture for the reader

Sensory Details
Explain sights, sounds, smells, tastes, and feelings

Closing Sentence
Wraps up the paragraph

My Nana's house is the best place to dunk cookies and basketballs. As soon as you open the door, you **smell** Nana's **sweet** oatmeal cookies. Inside are dozens of **pictures** of my family. My favorite one is from Nana's trip to Alaska. It's a **photo** of her riding a dog sled! Our next stop is the kitchen. There, we have **warm, chewy** cookies and **ice cold** milk. Behind the house, Nana teaches me how to shoot hoops. She still has a perfect free throw. She never misses! I think all the neighbors can hear her **laugh and cheer** every time she sinks one. She **holds** my hands and helps me aim at the hoop. My **heart races** every time. After dinner, Nana drives me home. I never want to leave her house, but I love getting a ride in her cool old convertible!

The Five Senses
Touch
Taste
Sight
Smell
Sound

Follow your teacher's directions to complete Frames 1 and 2.

**We Do
1** There's no place in the world like _____

_____. As soon as you open the door, _____

(see) _____.

_____

_____. (smell) _____

_____. (feel) _____

_____

_____.

**You Do
2** _____

_____

_____. (see) _____

_____

_____. _____

_____

_____. (smell) _____

_____

_____.

**You Do
3** On a separate sheet of paper, use your prewriting plan
to write a description, or make a new plan to write
about your favorite outdoor place.

Dialogue

Dialogue is the words spoken by characters. These words help tell the story and share the thoughts and feelings of the characters.

Parts of Dialogue

- The names of the characters who are speaking
- Interesting details that show the thoughts of the characters and help to tell the story
- Quotation marks

pencils

My Day in Court

Last summer, I got to go to work with my mom to see exactly what she does all day. It was awesome! You see, my mom is a judge, so I got to spend the day watching a trial in her courtroom. I learned a lot but also had a few questions for her at the end of the day.

Characters
Names show which character is speaking

"How do people get to be on the jury?" I asked.

Quotation Marks
Show the characters' exact words

"People in our city take turns being on a jury," Mom explained. "First, they get a letter in the mail telling when to come to court. When they get there, they answer a few questions. Then, some people are asked to be on the jury for a few days or maybe even a week or more."

Details
Show the characters' feelings and help readers get to know them better

"That would be the most exciting week ever!" I said.

Words for Dialogue
Said
Replied
Answered
Told
Asked
Questioned
Exclaimed
Cried

"You'll have a turn someday," Mom told me.

I can't wait to go back to court. Maybe one day I'll be on a jury. Maybe I'll even be a judge, like my mom.

Name _____

Follow your teacher's directions to complete the frame.

1 One of the most exciting days I ever had was _____

_____.

My friend said, "_____

_____

_____."

" _____

_____

_____!" I exclaimed.

" _____

_____.

_____," she told me.

Then, _____

_____

We both cried, "_____

_____!"

2 On a separate sheet of paper, write about a time when you used clues to solve a problem. Include dialogue in your writing.

3 On a separate sheet of paper, use your prewriting plan to write a piece that includes dialogue, or make a new plan to write about a time when you did something new.

Personal Narrative

A **personal narrative** is a true story about something that happened to the writer. A personal narrative about the writer's life may also be called an autobiography.

Parts of a Personal Narrative

- A beginning that grabs readers' interest
- Events that really happened to the writer, told in time order, or sequence
- Interesting details that elaborate events and the writer's feelings
- Use of the pronoun *I*
- An ending that tells how the story worked out and how the writer felt about it

pencils

Beginning
Makes readers want to find out more

Events
Tell what happened in time order

Interesting Details
Include sights, sounds, and feelings

Ending
Wraps up the story and tells how the writer felt

When I danced in my first talent show last year, I got a big surprise! It all started when the red curtains opened. Rows of kids sat looking up at me. I stood really still and waited for the music to come on. **At first,** I just worried about messing up my moves. **Then** I had something else to worry about. The music didn't start! I panicked. I ran off the stage to where Mrs. Meeks had the equipment. The computer battery had died. Suddenly I had an idea. I dug my MP3 player out of my backpack. We plugged it into the speakers, and my song started blasting! **Finally,** I ran back onstage and danced like nothing had happened. I guess I did okay, because everyone cheered at the end. Whew, what a close call!

Other Transitions
First
Next
After that
During
After a while
Meanwhile
Later
Last

Name _____

Follow your teacher's directions to complete Frames 1 and 2.

1 One of the hardest things I ever did was _____

_____ .

At first, _____

_____

_____ . Then _____

_____

_____ . Finally, _____

_____ .

When it was over, I felt _____

_____ .

2 _____

_____ .

_____ . First, _____

_____ .

_____ . After that, _____

_____ .

_____ . Finally, _____

_____ .

3 On a separate sheet of paper, use your prewriting plan
to write a personal narrative, or make a new plan to
write about something you did that made you proud.

Personal Narrative: Prewriting

A **personal narrative** tells a true story about something that happened to the author. Before you write a personal narrative, you should prewrite to brainstorm and plan your ideas.

Prewriting

- First, brainstorm a list of possible topics. For a personal narrative, think about interesting things that have happened to you or things you have done.
- Then, choose an event you would like to share with readers. Use a graphic organizer to plan the interesting details to include.

Topic brainstorming

School talent show

Backyard campout with Dad

Flying on an airplane

Event: We set up the tent in the backyard.
Details: tent fell down twice before we finished
      dog wanted to lay down inside the tent

Event: We made a fire in the fire pit.
Details: roasted hot dogs and marshmallows for dinner
      some marshmallows caught fire

Event: My dad and I slept in the tent all night.
Details: sleeping bags were warm and comfortable
      heard owls during the night

Name _____

Follow your teacher's directions to complete this page.

1 **Topic:** A time I did something with someone special

> **Event:**
>
> **Details:**

↓

> **Event:**
>
> **Details:**

↓

> **Event:**
>
> **Details:**

2 On a separate sheet of paper, fill in a graphic organizer like the one above to plan a personal narrative. Write details about a time you learned to do something new.

3 On a separate sheet of paper, prewrite a personal narrative. You can also use what you have learned to make an old plan better.

Personal Narrative

A **personal narrative** is a story about the writer's experiences. It tells his or her thoughts and feelings.

Parts of a Personal Narrative

- A beginning that gets readers interested
- Time clues that show the order of events
- Details that are grouped together in a way that makes sense
- An ending that tells how the story worked out

Beginning
Catches the readers' interest so they want to keep reading

Details
Tell the events in order and are grouped with other details about the same thing

Time Clues
Help show when events happen or how long they last

Ending
Tells how everything worked out

A Night Under the Stars

Last spring, my dad and I had the most amazing campout ever. The best part was that we never left home. We had a campout in the backyard. As soon as I got home from school, we started to set up the tent. That was kind of tricky. The tent fell down twice before we got it finished. We laughed so hard I almost fell down, too! Once that was done, Dad made a fire. We used some of the wood for our fireplace. We cooked hot dogs on the fire, and then we toasted marshmallows. Mom came out and cooked with us, too. Her marshmallows kept catching fire, so Dad shared with her. When Mom went in the house, Dad and I crawled into the tent. We heard owls hooting, so we decided to tell spooky stories. Finally we fell asleep. We both slept great. It was the perfect campout!

Other Words that Tell Time Order
Before that
Earlier in the day
First
Later
Meanwhile
Soon
When I was younger

Name _____

Follow your teacher's directions to complete this page.

1 When I was younger, I got to _____

with _____ .

First, _____

_____

_____

_____

Later _____

_____

_____

_____

Eventually, _____

_____

_____

The best part was _____

_____

_____

_____ .

2 On a separate sheet of paper, write a personal narrative about a time you learned to do something new.

3 On a separate sheet of paper, use your prewriting plan to write a personal narrative, or make a new plan to write about your most exciting day.

Response Paragraph

A **response paragraph** is writing that tells about what you have read and what you think about it.

Parts of a Response Paragraph

- An interesting opening
- A topic sentence that mentions the title
- Details and examples that tell something about the selection. For a story, they tell about the characters or what happens.
- The writer's thoughts, feelings, and ideas about the selection

Topic Sentence
Includes the title

Details and Examples
Tell about the selection

Writer's thoughts and feelings

Transitions
Show time order or link ideas

Have your parents ever said you are too picky? Well, I would tell you and them to read <u>Goldilocks: A Modern Tale</u>. In that story, Goldie is just too hard to please. **To start with**, Goldie becomes a judge on a cooking show. She tastes three kinds of pizza. She says Dad Bear's pizza is icky because it has too much sauce. **Then** she dislikes the cheese on Mom Bear's pizza. When she tastes Kid Bear's peanut butter pizza she says, "Hmm. This is pretty odd." **Later**, she wins a trip to the mountains. The bears loan her some skis. I thought she would be happy, but she was not. She says they are the wrong color! She does not even say "Thank you." I could not believe that she was so rude. **In the end**, Goldie learns not to be so picky. She even starts to like peanut butter pizza! I thought <u>Goldilocks: A Modern Tale</u> was a great book!

Other Transitions
First of all
Second
Plus
Another
So
Finally

Name _____

Follow your teacher's directions to complete the frame.

We Do
1   In the story _____

_____

_____.

To start with, _____

_____

_____. Then _____

_____

_____

_____.

Later, _____

_____

_____. In the end, _____

_____

_____

_____.

You Do
2   On another sheet of paper, write a response paragraph about another book you have read. Remember to give details from the book as well as your feelings about it.

You Do
3   On a separate sheet of paper, use your prewriting plan to write a response paragraph, or make a new plan to write about how another character changed during a story.

Opinion Paragraph

An **opinion paragraph** tells what the writer thinks about a topic. It explains why he or she has this view.

Parts of an Opinion Paragraph

- A topic sentence that introduces the writer's opinion
- Reasons that support the point of view
- Linking words that connect the opinion to reasons
- A concluding statement that ties ideas together

Topic Sentence
Tells how the writer feels about the topic

Reasons
Explain why the writer has this opinion

Linking Words
Connect the opinion to the reasons

Conclusion
Restates the writer's opinion

Jack and the Beanstalk

Jack and the Beanstalk is the best fairy tale ever. One reason this is my favorite story is because so many things happen to Jack that never happen in real life. **For example**, who ever really gets to trade a cow for magic beans? That would be an amazing trade! **Another reason** this story is the greatest is that Jack gets to climb a huge beanstalk. **Since** I love to climb trees, I imagine climbing a beanstalk that is higher than the clouds would be so much fun. Also, Jack gets to have an adventure in a new place when he climbs into the sky. Going to someplace new is always exciting, **so** meeting a giant in his land would be so cool! I wish I could do all of the things Jack does. **That is why** I think *Jack and the Beanstalk* is the best fairy tale.

Linking Words
Because
Due to
For example
For this reason
Since
So
Therefore

Name _____

Follow your teacher's directions to complete the frame.

1 One of the best books I have ever read was

_____.

I like it because _____

_____

_____

_____

_____. For example _____

_____

_____

_____

_____.

So _____

_____

_____. That is why _____

_____

_____.

2 On a separate sheet of paper, write an opinion paragraph about your favorite art activity.

3 On a separate sheet of paper, use your prewriting plan to write an opinion paragraph, or make a new plan to write about a job that you might like to have someday.

Response Paragraph

A **response paragraph** tells the writer's answer to a question or a prompt. Sometimes, the response answers a question about a story.

Parts of a Response Paragraph

- A topic sentence that uses words from the prompt
- Details and examples that explain the writer's ideas
- Quotation marks that go around a speaker's exact words

Topic Sentence
Words from the prompt show what question is being answered

Details and Examples
Explain the writer's ideas

Quotation Marks
Show any exact words from the story

The Harvest Birds

Prompt: How do you think the people in town felt about Juan at the end of the story?

At the end of the story, I think the townspeople started to feel respect for Juan. One thing that shows this is when the story says, "When Juan arrived in town, everyone was amazed." They saw that he was a great farmer because he had such a wonderful harvest. They were surprised he was able to grow so much food. Next, some of them even asked for his advice. They said, "Teach me your secrets!" Some other people even offered to give him a job. They were not laughing at him now. They respected him and wanted him to work for them.

Other Transitions
First
Then
After that
During
After a while
Later
Last
Finally

Name _____

Follow your teacher's directions to complete the frame.

1 **Prompt: Why do you think Juan had such a great harvest?**

I think Juan had a great harvest because _____

_____.

At first, _____

_____

_____

_____. Then, _____

_____

_____

_____. In the story, it says, "_____

_____

_____"

Last, _____

_____

_____.

2 On a separate sheet of paper, write a response paragraph to answer the following: What do you think would be the best part of working as an illustrator?

3 On a separate sheet of paper, use your prewriting plan to write a response paragraph, or make a new plan to answer the following prompt: Why are pictures important to a story?

Response to Literature: Prewriting

A **response to literature** answers a prompt or question about a story.

Prewriting

- Begin by listing your ideas about the prompt.
- Then, choose which idea to write about. Use a graphic organizer to plan the details, examples, and quotes to use in your response.

Prompt: Why do you think Jiichan wanted to be the kamishibai man again?

Topic brainstorming

He enjoyed riding his bike to the city

He hoped to see the grown-up kids again

He liked being around the kids

Opinion: I think Jiichan wanted to be the kamishibai man again because he liked being with kids.

Reason: He must like kids because he and his wife called each other Grandma and Grandpa.
Details: "Even though they never had children of their own, they called each other 'Jiichan' and 'Baachan'. Jiichan is Grandpa, and Baachan is Grandma."

Reason: He was excited to go back to the city to see the kids.
Details: hummed a tune as he rode his bike to town

Reason: He called the kids and gave them candy when they came to hear the stories.
Details: yelled and used clappers to get their attention; knew which candy they liked best

---

Name _____

Follow your teacher's directions to complete this page.

 1 **Prompt:** What would you most enjoy about someone like the kamishibai man?

Opinion:
Reason:
Details:
Reason:
Details:
Reason:
Details:

2 On a separate sheet of paper, fill in a graphic organizer like the one above. Write your ideas for a response to literature for the prompt: What would you most enjoy about someone like the kamishibai man? Think about reasons and details to support your opinion.

3 On a separate sheet of paper, prewrite a response to literature. You can also use what you have learned to make an old plan better.

Response to Literature

A **response to literature** explains the writer's ideas about a story. It answers a question or prompt about the text.

✏ Parts of a Response to Literature

- A topic sentence that includes some words from the prompt and tells the writer's opinion
- Details and examples that support the writer's ideas
- Exact words from the story in quotation marks
- Linking words that connect the opinion and details
- A clear conclusion that wraps up the ideas

Topic Sentence
Repeats words from the prompt and tells the main idea

Linking Words
Connect the writer's opinion to the supporting details

Details
Support the opinion

Conclusion
Wraps up the ideas

Prompt: Why do you think Jiichan wanted to be the kamishibai man again?

I think Jiichan wanted to be the kamishibai man again because he enjoyed being with the kids. He must have liked kids, since he and his wife called each other Grandma and Grandpa. The story said, "Even though they never had children of their own, they called each other 'Jiichan' and 'Baachan,'" which mean Grandma and Grandpa. He was so excited to see the kids that he hummed a tune as he rode his bike to town. He also gave the kids their favorite candy. Only someone who really likes kids would learn what candy is their favorite. Jiichan wanted to be the kamishibai man again because he wanted to be with the kids again.

Other Linking Words
Because
For example
For this reason
Since
So
Therefore

Name _____

Follow your teacher's directions to complete this page.

1 **Prompt:** What would you most enjoy about seeing someone like the kamishibai man?

The thing I would most enjoy about seeing someone like the

kamishibai man is _____

_____

_____ .

The story said _____

_____

_____

_____ .

Also, _____

_____

_____

_____

_____ .

2 On a separate sheet of paper, write a response to literature to answer the prompt: What would you most enjoy about seeing someone like the kamishibai man?

3 On a separate sheet of paper, use your prewriting plan to write a response to literature, or make a new plan to answer the following prompt: What do you think caused Jiichan to change from the beginning of the story to the end?

Cause and Effect Paragraphs

Cause and effect paragraphs explain causes, or why something happens. They also explain effects, or what happens. Some events have more than one cause or effect.

Parts of Cause and Effect Paragraphs

- An introduction that tells the main cause or effect
- One or more causes
- One or more effects
- Transition words that help show the causes and effects
- Details from two or more texts that explain the causes and effects

Introduction
Tells the main effect

Every year, many birds migrate, or fly south for the winter. How do they know when it is time to go? Do they have calendars in their nests? No. Scientists have a few different ideas about **why** birds fly south.

Causes
Tell the reason or reasons something happened

According to *Birds,* some scientists think **cold weather makes birds** migrate south. In cold weather, there are not as many plants, fruits, or insects for birds to eat. **Because of this**, birds fly to

Effects
Tell other events that happen as a result

where the weather is warmer and there is more food.

According to *The Bird Encyclopedia,* scientists think birds migrate **because** days grow shorter in the fall. When there is less sunlight, birds eat more food, which gives them extra energy.

Other Transitions
So
Since
After that
The reason for

Details
Explain causes and effects

These scientists say that **this energy tells birds** to take off and begin their migration.

Name _____

Follow your teacher's directions to complete the frame.

1   Dinosaurs ruled the Earth for millions of years, but they are no longer around. Different scientists have different ideas about what made the dinosaurs extinct.

_____

_____

_____ why _____

_____

_____

_____ caused _____

_____

_____

_____. As a result, _____

_____

_____. _____ because

_____

_____

_____ .

2 Why are airplanes so important? On a separate sheet of paper, write at least two effects of the invention of the airplane. Use at least two sources to find facts.

3 On a separate sheet of paper, plan and write about what causes food to spoil. Give two or more possible causes. Use at least two sources.

Compare and Contrast Paragraphs

Compare and contrast paragraphs tell how two things are alike and different. Details help explain the similarities and differences.

Parts of Compare and Contrast Paragraphs

- An introduction tells what will be compared and contrasted
- Details tell how the subjects are alike and different
- Linking words connect the ideas
- A conclusion sums up the paragraph

Introduction
Tells the subjects of the paragraph

Details
Show how the subjects are the same and how they are different

Linking Words
Show how ideas are connected

Conclusion
Wraps up the ideas in the paragraph

Earth and Mars

In science today, we learned that Mars is like Earth in some ways but different in other ways.

Both planets orbit, or travel around, the sun. Like Earth, Mars has four seasons. Another way the planets are alike is that Earth and Mars have about the same amount of dry land.

However, Mars is only about half as big around as Earth. So, most of Mars is desert, but most of Earth is covered with water. The biggest difference is that humans can live on Earth. Humans can't breathe the air on Mars, so we can't live there.

So, even though the planets are alike in some ways, there are important differences between Earth and Mars.

Other Words to Compare and Contrast
Alike
Differ from
However
Unlike
Same
Similar
On the other hand

Name _____

Follow your teacher's directions to complete the frame.

Two subjects we have learned about this year are _____

_____ and _____.

One thing these have in common is _____

_____

_____

_____. Another _____

_____

_____

However, _____

_____

_____

Unlike _____

_____

_____

So, _____

_____

On a separate sheet of paper, write paragraphs that
compare and contrast two story characters.

On a separate sheet of paper, use your prewriting plan
to write compare and contrast paragraphs, or make a
new plan to write about two activities you enjoy.

Informative Paragraph

An **informative paragraph** includes facts about a topic. It is written to teach or share true information.

✏️ Parts of an Informative Paragraph

- A topic sentence that introduces the main idea
- Facts and examples that support and explain the main idea
- True information that teaches about the topic

Topic Sentence
Introduces the main idea and tells what the paragraph is about

Supporting Details
Facts and examples explain the main idea

True Information
Teaches readers about the topic

Appalachian Mountains

The Appalachian (a-puh-LATCH-un) Mountains make up a huge, important mountain range. A *mountain range* is a row of mountains that are connected. The Appalachian Mountains are about 300 miles wide and 2,000 miles long. They run from Alabama to Canada. That is almost the whole length of the U.S. The mountains' highest point is in North Carolina. It is almost 7,000 feet tall, which is more than one mile high! One reason these mountains are important is that they divide the eastern and western parts of the U.S. They are also important because they were home to many Native American tribes. The mountains were named after the Apalachee Indians, who lived in what is now Florida. The Appalachian Mountains have been important to the United States for hundreds of years.

Other Transitions
First
Second
Next
Also
In addition
For example
Finally

Name _____

Follow your teacher's directions to complete the frame.

1 An important leader of the United States was _____

_____. One reason _____

_____

_____

_____

Another _____

_____

_____

_____. Also _____

_____

_____

_____. Finally, _____

_____

_____

2 On a separate sheet of paper, write an informative paragraph about a place you have visited.

3 On a separate sheet of paper, use your prewriting plan to write an informative paragraph, or make a new plan to write about something or someone you have learned about in class.

Explanatory Essay: Prewriting

An **explanatory essay** tells *what*, *why*, or *how* about a topic. It uses facts and details to explain the topic.

✏ Prewriting

- For an explanatory essay, begin by listing ideas for a topic. Think of things about which you would like to explain *what*, *how*, or *why*.
- Next, narrow the topic by selecting something specific about it to explore. Then, create an outline to organize facts.

Topic brainstorming

- pets
- cool jobs
- police dogs

Narrowing the Topic

pets

learning about pets

how to get ready for

a new pet

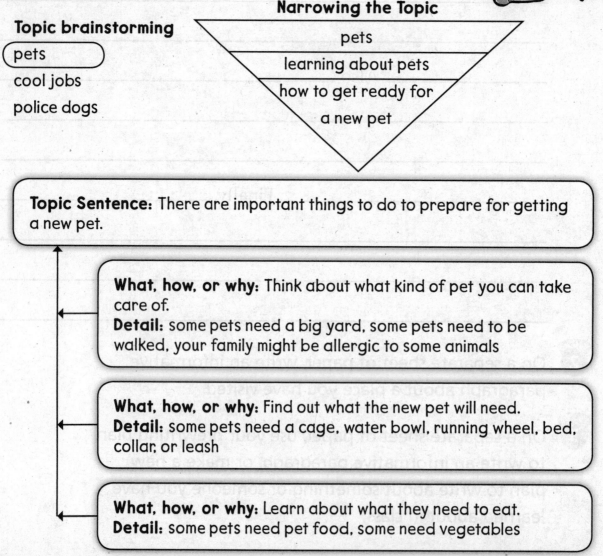

Topic Sentence: There are important things to do to prepare for getting a new pet.

What, how, or why: Think about what kind of pet you can take care of.
Detail: some pets need a big yard, some pets need to be walked, your family might be allergic to some animals

What, how, or why: Find out what the new pet will need.
Detail: some pets need a cage, water bowl, running wheel, bed, collar, or leash

What, how, or why: Learn about what they need to eat.
Detail: some pets need pet food, some need vegetables

Name _____

Follow your teacher's directions to complete this page.

 1 **Prompt:** Think about a job you might like to have one day. Explain why this would be a great job for you.

> **Topic Sentence:**

>> **What, how, or why:**
>>
>> **Detail:**

>> **What, how, or why:**
>>
>> **Detail:**

>> **What, how, or why:**
>>
>> **Detail:**

 2 On a separate sheet of paper, fill in a graphic organizer like the one above. Write your ideas for an explanatory essay about how to do something. Make sure it is something you know well. Think about what the activity it is, how to do it, or why you enjoy the activity. Use details to explain each of the ideas.

 3 On a separate sheet of paper, prewrite an explanatory essay. You can also use what you have learned to make an old plan better.

Explanatory Essay

An **explanatory essay** explains *what*, *how*, or *why* about something. Facts, definitions, and details tell about the topic.

Parts of an Explanatory Essay

- A topic sentence that introduces the main idea
- Details, facts and definitions that explain the topic
- Information that is grouped together in a way that makes sense
- Linking words that connect ideas
- A conclusion that sums up the essay

Topic Sentence
Introduces the topic and tells the main idea

Linking Words
Connect details to the main idea

Details, Facts, and Definitions
Help to explain the topic and support the main idea

Conclusion
Sums up the essay

Preparing for a Pet

Are you thinking about adding a new animal friend to your family? If so, there are a few important things to do to prepare for getting a new pet.

First, think about what kind of pet you can take care of. For example, is your yard big enough to keep a pony? Is someone able to walk a dog while you are at school? Make sure you choose a pet that is best for your family.

Also, find out what your pet will need. For instance, a hamster will need a cage, a water bottle, and a running wheel. A puppy will need a collar and a leash. Finally, find out what kind of food your pet needs. Pets need to eat the right kinds of things to stay healthy

To be a good pet owner, you will need to be ready for your new friend.

Linking Words
And
Another reason
More
But
In addition

Name _____

Follow your teacher's directions to complete this page.

A job that I might like to have one day is _____.

One reason this would be a great job for me is _____

_____

_____

_____. For example, _____

_____

_____

_____.

In addition, _____

_____

_____

_____.

In the end, _____ is the perfect job for me because

_____

_____.

On a separate sheet of paper, write an explanatory essay about something that you are good at doing.

On a separate sheet of paper, use your prewriting plan to write an explanatory essay, or make a new plan to write about what makes someone a good friend.

Persuasive Letter

A **persuasive letter** is written to convince someone to agree with the writer's ideas. It explains the writer's views about a subject.

✎ Parts of a Persuasive Letter

- A goal that is stated at the beginning
- Strong reasons that support the goal
- Correct letter form with a heading, inside address, greeting, body, closing, and signature
- Language that is positive and polite

Correct Letter Form
Has heading, inside address, greeting, body, closing, and signature

Goal
Tells what the writer wants the audience to do

Reasons
Show why the writer believes in the goal

Language
Sounds positive and polite

387 Oak Hill Drive
Branford, FL 32008
December 18, 2012

432 East Lake Street
Branford, FL 32008

Dear Mr. Harper,

  Our class would like you to give us permission to begin a recycling program in the school cafeteria. The trash cans are full of things that could be recycled. We want to have separate bins for paper, cans, and plastic bottles. Everyone can put things in the bins when they leave the lunchroom. It would be very simple. Please allow us to begin this program because we should all do our part to save the Earth.

                    Sincerely,
                    Madison Lopez

Persuasive Words
Need to
Should
Important
Please
Best
Must

Name _____

Follow your teacher's directions to complete the frame.

_____

_____

_____

_____

_____

Dear _____,

We would like to _____

_____

_____

_____

_____

_____

_____.

Sincerely,

_____

 On a separate sheet of paper, write a persuasive letter to your teacher or principal.

 On a separate sheet of paper, use your prewriting plan to write a persuasive letter, or make a new plan to write a persuasive letter to your parents.

Opinion Paragraph

An **opinion paragraph** tells what the writer thinks about a topic. It also explains why the writer has this view.

Parts of an Opinion Paragraph

- A clear, interesting topic sentence that tells the writer's opinion
- Strong reasons that support the writer's opinion
- Interesting, convincing details that explain the reasons
- A closing sentence that repeats the opinion or makes a final comment

pencils

Topic Sentence
Introduces the writer's opinion

Reasons
Tell why the writer feels the way he or she does about the topic

Details
Explain the reasons

Closing Sentence
Repeats the opinion in a new way

A Day at the Museum

The science museum was the best field trip we took this year. One reason is because there were so many cool things to see there. For example, there was a real dinosaur skeleton. It was almost as tall as the roof. It was amazing to find out what it would feel like to stand beside one of these animals. We also got to do some neat activities. One thing we did was make fossils out of clay. I used a leaf. I pressed the leaf into the clay, and then I lifted it out. The leaf left a print in the clay, kind of like a fossil. Finally, we looked at bones from different animals. We used clues and pictures to figure out what animals they were from. The science museum was by far the most awesome trip we took all year!

Other Transitions
First
Second
Next
Another
Then
In addition

Name _____

Follow your teacher's directions to complete the frame.

1 The best school assembly we had was _____

_____.

The first reason _____

_____

_____

_____

_____. Another reason _____

_____.

_____

_____

_____

_____. Also _____

_____

_____

_____.

2 On a separate sheet of paper, write an opinion paragraph about an animal that you think would make a great pet.

3 On a separate sheet of paper, use your prewriting plan to write an opinion paragraph, or make a new plan to write about something you think would be interesting to study.

Problem and Solution Paragraph

A **problem and solution paragraph** states a problem and a possible way to solve the problem.

Parts of a Problem and Solution Paragraph

- A problem that is clearly stated at the beginning
- A possible solution that is given
- Reasons, facts, and examples that support the solution and persuade readers to agree with it
- Exact words that explain the problem and solution

pencils

Problem
Introduced at the beginning

Possible Solution
Tells one way to solve the problem

Reasons, Facts, and Examples
Explain how the solution would be helpful

Tree Trouble

Our family enjoys camping in the woods, but we do not always know the names of the plants and trees we see there. This can be a major problem. Can you imagine walking through poison ivy because you do not know what it is? Itchy! One way to solve this problem is to take a nature guidebook with us. It shows pictures of different plants and tells about each one. A guidebook can teach us which plants are poisonous. Plus, we can read about which types of tree branches are best for making a campfire. For example, wood from spruce trees makes a lot of smoke. It can also throw sparks, which is not safe. A guidebook can teach us about the plants and help to keep us safe when we are camping.

Other Transitions
First
Second
Third
In addition
As well as
Another way
For instance

Name _____

Follow your teacher's directions to complete the frame.

We Do 1   Our family likes to _____, but one problem we

face is _____

_____.

We could solve this by _____

_____

_____

_____. The first reason _____

_____

_____.

Another _____.

_____

_____

_____. For example, _____

_____

_____

_____.

You Do 2   On a separate sheet of paper, write a problem and
solution paragraph about a game or activity you do
with friends.

You Do 3   On a separate sheet of paper, use your prewriting plan
to write a problem and solution paragraph, or make a
new plan to write about a chore you do at home.

Persuasive Essay: Prewriting

A **persuasive essay** gives reasons, facts, and examples to convince the reader to agree with a writer's opinion.

Prewriting

- First, brainstorm possible topics. Think about topics that you have an opinion about and list them.
- Next, select a topic that you would like to convince readers to agree with. Use a graphic organizer to choose which ideas to include in your essay.

Topic brainstorming

Eating a healthy breakfast

Cleaning up our community

Getting enough exercise

> **Opinion:**
> It is important to get enough exercise.

> **Reason:** It is good for your body.
> **Details:** Helps heart and muscles, and keeps you from getting sick

> **Reason:** It helps your brain.
> **Details:** Keeps you awake and gives you extra energy

> **Reason:** It is fun.
> **Details:** Can choose an exercise that you like to do with your friends

Name _____

Follow your teacher's directions to complete this page.

1 **Topic:** Something I think is important for kids to do

> **Opinion:**
>
> > **Reason:**
> >
> > **Details:**
>
> > **Reason:**
> >
> > **Details:**
>
> > **Reason:**
> >
> > **Details:**

2 On a separate sheet of paper, fill in a graphic organizer like the one above. Write your ideas for a persuasive essay. Think about your beliefs and opinions about school. Then, write about why it is important to learn your favorite subject.

3 On a separate sheet of paper, prewrite a persuasive essay. You can also use what you have learned to make an old plan better.

Persuasive Essay

A **persuasive essay** is an essay that gives a writer's opinion as well as reasons to support that opinion.

Parts of a Persuasive Essay

- The writer's opinion or goal
- Reasons why the reader should agree with the writer
- Linking words to connect an opinion with reasons
- Facts and examples that elaborate the reasons
- A closing that wraps up the writer's goal and reasons

Introduction
Tells the writer's goal or opinion

Reasons
Tell why readers should agree with the writer

Facts and Examples
Explain the reasons

Closing
Wraps up the writer's goals and reasons

If you want to feel great and have fun, I know how. Exercise! If you exercise even a little every day, you will feel better and have a great time.

First of all, exercise is good for your body because it makes your muscles and bones healthy. Therefore, it helps keep your heart healthy, too. **Another reason** to exercise is that keeping your body active will help keep your mind active, too. This might help you pay more attention in school. You may even get better grades! **Finally, the best reason** to exercise is that it is a lot of fun! Playing soccer, dancing, swimming, and jumping rope are all great ways to exercise.

You can have fun and stay fit if you exercise more. Exercise is not only a great way to stay healthy, it's a great way to stay happy.

Other Transitions
To start with
One reason
The second reason
In addition
Also
After a while
As well as
Later
Last

Name _____

Follow your teacher's directions to complete the frame.

1   Everyone should join a sports team.

The first reason is _____

_____

_____

_____.

A third reason is _____

_____

_____

_____. Finally, the best reason is _____

_____

_____

_____

_____

2   On a separate sheet of paper, write a persuasive essay about why people should attend a concert or sporting event.

3   On a separate sheet of paper, use your prewriting plan to write a persuasive essay, or make a new plan to write about why people should visit your local park.

Fictional Narrative Paragraph

A **fictional narrative paragraph** is a short story about make believe characters and events. It includes characters, a problem, and a solution.

Parts of a Fictional Narrative Paragraph

- A beginning that catches the readers' interest
- Characters who face a problem
- Timeorder transition words that tell the order of events
- Suspense that makes readers curious about what might happen

Beginning
Gets the readers' interest

Problem
What the character has to face

Vivid Words
Describe what characters see, feel, and hear

Suspense
Makes readers curious

Abe's Big Game

Today Abe was going to play ice hockey for the first time, and he was afraid everyone would laugh at him if he messed up. He walked with his friends to the frozen lake. It was freezing outside, and the ice-cold air stung his face. **As soon as** they got there and his skates were tied, Abe stepped onto the lake. His felt his feet start to slip. **Then** he got his balance and began to skate. **Before long**, the game was tied. **Then** it happened. The puck was coming straight toward him. If he made the goal, his team would win. Abe's heart thumped. He swung his hockey stick. Smack! Abe made the winning shot! He couldn't wait to play again.

Other Time Order Transitions
At the beginning
First
Next
In no time
After that
Soon
While
Later

Name _____

Follow your teacher's directions to complete the frame.

1 _____

_____

_____

To begin with, _____

_____

_____

_____

_____. After that, _____

_____

_____

_____

_____. By the end _____

_____

_____

 2 On a separate sheet of paper, write a fictional narrative paragraph about a character who wants to learn something new.

3 On a separate sheet of paper, use your prewriting plan to write a fictional narrative paragraph, or make a new plan to write about someone who faces a challenge.

Descriptive Paragraph

A **descriptive paragraph** explains what something is like. It creates a clear picture of the topic for the readers.

Parts of a Descriptive Paragraph

- A topic that is introduced at the beginning
- Words and details that show the writer's feelings
- Sensory details that tell how something looks, sounds, feels, tastes, or smells
- Similes that help explain what something is like
- Ideas that are organized in a clear order

Topic
Tells what the story is about

Similes
Describe what something is like

Sensory Details
Tell about the sights, sounds, smells, tastes, and feelings

Words and Details
Show the feelings of the writer

Speckles' Surprise

Yesterday I got the best surprise ever! The smell of bacon and pancakes woke me up early. My mom always makes my favorite breakfast on special days. I hopped out of bed and threw on my soft, fluffy robe. I skipped into the kitchen right away. While I chomped down the last bite of sweet, sticky, maple syrup-covered pancake, Mom said she had a special surprise for me. Her eyes were sparkling like glitter, so I knew it had to be something amazing. Just then I heard a scratch-scratch-scratch on the back door. Mom smiled and nodded. I was so excited that I threw the door open as fast as lightning, and it hit the wall with a loud BAM! My dog, Speckles, stood there, looking up at me with her round, dark eyes. Then I saw the tiny little balls of fur inside her dog house. Speckles had puppies!

Other Sensory Details
Glowing
Warm
Icy
Snap
Light
Squeaky
Feathery
Salty

Name _____

Follow your teacher's directions to complete the frame.

We Do 1   The best day I ever had was _____

_____.

I heard _____

_____

_____ . The smell of _____

_____

_____

_____.

I saw _____

_____

_____

_____

_____.

You Do 2   On a separate sheet of paper, write a descriptive paragraph about something that made you happy.

You Do 3   On a separate sheet of paper, use your prewriting plan to write a descriptive paragraph, or make a new plan to write about a great surprise.

Dialogue

Dialogue is the words spoken by characters in a story. The dialogue helps to tell what is happening in a funny, exciting, or scary way.

Parts of a Dialogue

- Language that shows the personalities and feelings of the characters
- Formal and informal words that show characters' personalities
- Different types of sentences that make the dialogue sound interesting and natural

Different Kinds of Sentences
Statements, questions, commands, and exclamations make the writing sound natural

Language
Characters speak in a way that shows their personalities and feelings

Formal and Informal Words
Show characters' personalities

Laura couldn't wait to meet the new friend Uncle Mark was bringing to dinner. Soon, the doorbell rang. Laura ran to open the door. "What in the world is on your shoulder?" yelled Laura.

"This, my dear, is Melvin," explained Uncle Mark. "He's my monkey."

"Pleasure to meet ya," Laura said to Melvin. She leaned close to her uncle. "My mom is gonna flip out, you know. I can't wait to see this!"

Uncle Mark and Melvin followed Laura into the kitchen. "Hey, Mom," she said. "Look who's here."

Her mom turned around, and her mouth dropped open. "Well," she said politely, "now I know why you asked for banana cream pie for dessert."

Other Examples of Informal Words
Hey
Let's
We've
Yeah
Hang out
So long
What's up?

Name _____

Follow your teacher's directions to complete the frame.

1 No one had expected what was about to happen when _____

_____

_____. At first, _____

_____

_____. Then _____

" _____?"

asked _____.

" _____

_____

_____," suggested _____.

" _____

_____," whispered _____.

After that, _____

_____

" _____!" exclaimed _____.

2 On a separate sheet of paper, write dialogue about a character who is surprised by something.

3 On a separate sheet of paper, use your prewriting plan to write a dialogue, or make a new plan to write about characters who are afraid.

Fictional Narrative: Prewriting

A fictional narrative is a made-up story that tells about characters who solve a problem. It has a plot told in time order.

Prewriting

- First, brainstorm a list of possible plots.
- Next, choose a plot to write about. Use a graphic organizer to list ideas for setting, characters, and events.

Topic brainstorming

Staying safe in a storm

A family's first earthquake

What happened when a town flooded

Setting	Characters
Home	Jada, Jada's Mom

Plot
Beginning: An emergency signal is on the radio telling them that a bad rainstorm is coming.
Middle: The family waits in the kitchen where they will be safe.
End: The radio tells that the storm has turned and the weather is safe.

Name _____

Follow your teacher's directions to complete this page.

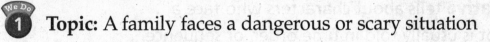

1 **Topic:** A family faces a dangerous or scary situation

Setting	Characters

Plot

Beginning:

Middle:

End:

2 On a separate sheet of paper, fill in a story map like the one above. Write your ideas for a fictional narrative. Think about planning for a big event. Then tell about someone getting ready for something that is about to happen.

3 On a separate sheet of paper, prewrite a fictional narrative. You can also use what you have learned to make an old plan better.

Fictional Narrative

A **fictional narrative** tells about characters who face a problem. The plot is usually told in time order, or sequence, and shows how the characters solve the problem.

✏ Parts of a Fictional Narrative

- A plot with a beginning, a middle, and an end
- Characters, a setting, and a problem that are introduced in the beginning
- Dialogue that shows characters' feelings
- Vivid details to create a clear picture for readers
- An end that shows how the problem is solved

Beginning
Introduces the characters, setting, and problem

Middle
Vivid details show how the characters work to solve the problem

Dialogue
Shows characters' feelings

End
Shows how the problem is solved

A loud, terrible noise from the TV filled Jada's room. "What is that screaming?" she asked.

"It's an emergency signal," Mom explained. **Just then**, a man's deep voice came on. He said there was a tornado warning.

"Oh no! What should we do?" Jada cried.

"We have to get in the closet," her mom said. She grabbed the radio from the kitchen counter. They dashed to Mom's bedroom closet. They huddled together on the floor.

"If there's a tornado, it is best to be away from doors and windows. We need to be in the middle of the house, not by the outside walls," Mom said. **While** they waited, they listened to the radio. **Soon**, the tornado passed.

"I am glad that's over," said Jada. "I would rather curl up on the couch than in the closet!"

Other Transitions
First
Next
After that
As
During
After a while
Meanwhile
Later
Finally

Name _____

Follow your teacher's directions to complete the frame.

1

_____

_____

_____. Just then, _____

_____

_____. While _____

_____. Soon, _____

_____.

_____

_____.

_____

_____

_____

_____. Following that, _____

_____

_____. Last, _____

_____.

2 On a separate sheet of paper, write a fictional narrative about some unusual weather.

3 On a separate sheet of paper, use your prewriting plan to write a story, or make a new plan for a story about a natural disaster or other unusual situation.

Compare and Contrast Paragraph

When you **compare and contrast** two texts, you explain how the texts are alike and how they are different.

✏️ Parts of a Compare and Contrast Paragraph

- A topic sentence that names the texts
- A stated main idea for each paragraph
- Sentences that tell how the texts are alike
- Sentences that tell how they are different
- A closing that sums up your ideas

Topic Sentence
Names the texts

Comparing Sentences
Tell how the texts are the same

Contrasting Sentences
Tell how the texts are different

Closing
Sums up what is important

Charlotte's Web and *The Trumpet of the Swan* are alike in some ways. They are alike because E. B. White wrote both books, and they are both about animals that talk. Another thing that is alike in both books is how smart the animals are. In each book a kid makes friends with the animals, too. The two books are different, too. *Charlotte's Web* is about a pig and a spider, and it happens on a farm. *Trumpet of the Swan* is about birds, and it happens in the wild. Also, the books are illustrated by different people. Still, I think they are more alike than different.

Other Transitions
In addition
Similar
As well
On the other hand
Neither

Name _____

Follow your teacher's directions to complete Frames 1 and 2.

We Do 1

In some ways, _____ and

_____ are alike. They both _____

_____.

They also _____

_____

_____

_____

_____.

You Do 2

Some things about the books are different, too. _____

_____

_____

_____

_____

_____

_____

I think _____

_____.

You Do 3

On a separate sheet of paper, write a compare and contrast paragraph about two books you have read.

Problem/Solution Paragraph

A **problem/solution paragraph** introduces a problem and then explains a possible way to solve it.

Parts of a Problem/Solution Paragraph

- A topic sentence that tells the problem
- Supporting sentences that give a possible solution
- Details that explain the solution
- Ideas that are explained in a logical order

pencils

You've Got the Power

Problem
Introduced at the beginning

Possible Solution
Tells one way to solve the problem

Reasons, Facts, and Examples
Explain how the solution would be helpful

Have you ever forgotten to turn off the power? Most people know that it is important to save electricity, but it is still easy to forget. One way to solve this is to use a timer. All you have to do is plug electric gadgets into the timer. Then set it for a certain time, kind of like an alarm clock. Everything plugged into it will turn off at that time. This is an easy solution because once the timer is set, you do not have to think about it again. Also, you will not have to worry about leaving electric gadgets turned on when you are away from home. For example, has your mom ever gotten in the car and asked if she turned off the iron or the coffee pot? If these were on a timer, she would not have to worry. A timer is a great solution for forgetting to turn off the power.

Other Transitions
The first way
The next thing
Third
In addition
As well as
Another reason
For instance

Name _____

Follow your teacher's directions to complete the frame.

1   One problem that kids face today is _____

_____.

This could be solved by _____

_____

_____. One reason _____

_____

_____

_____.

The next reason _____.

_____

_____. For example, _____

_____

_____

_____.

2   On a separate sheet of paper, write a problem/solution paragraph about a way to solve a problem related to pollution.

3   On a separate sheet of paper, use your prewriting plan to write a problem/solution paragraph, or make a new plan to write about a problem that you would like to solve with your own invention. Explain how your invention would solve the problem.

Instructions

Instructions teach the reader how to do or make something. They give all the steps the reader must follow.

✏️ Parts of Instructions

- A topic sentence that tells what the instructions will explain
- A sentence stating all of the materials and supplies needed
- Words that show the order of the steps
- Exact words and details that explain each step
- A closing sentence that tells why the instructions are important or useful

pencils

Topic Sentence
Introduces the main idea

Materials
Tell everything the reader needs

Order Words
Show the order in which the steps should be followed

Closing Sentence
Tells why the instructions are useful and fun

Have you ever wished for a snowstorm even when it's warm outside? Here is how to make snowflakes you can keep inside all year. You will need white paper and scissors. **First**, fold the paper in half several times. Fold it any way you like. You can fold it up and down, sideways, or corner to corner. **Then** use scissors to cut lots of shapes from each side. Cut different shapes, such as squares, diamonds, and squiggles. Be sure not to cut away all the folds. You will need some folded parts to hold the paper together. **After** you cut, open the paper. It will look like a lacy snowflake. Hang it anywhere you like. Make a few more and you will feel like you live in a big snow globe!

Other Transitions
The first thing
Second
Next
Once that is done
After a while
Following this
Third
Last

Name _____

Follow your teacher's directions to complete the frame.

1 Something that is a lot of fun to do is _____
_____. You will need _____
_____. First, _____
_____
_____
_____
_____
_____. Then _____
_____
_____. After _____
_____
_____
_____. Finally, _____
_____
_____.

2 On a separate sheet of paper, give instructions for
something that is easy to do or make. Remember to
include any materials you may need.

3 On a separate sheet of paper, use your prewriting plan
to write instructions, or make a new plan to write
instructions that explain something else you like to do.

Research Report: Prewriting

A **research report** uses facts from more than one source to explain a topic.

Prewriting

- First, brainstorm a list of topics that interest you.
- Next, choose a topic that you would like to learn about. Use a graphic organizer to plan the questions you would like to answer, and organize the information that will be included in the report.

Topic brainstorming

France

Killer Whales

Basketball

Topic: Basketball

> **Question:** Who invented basketball?
>
> **Details:** Dr. James Naismith (1861 – 1939) a gym teacher from Massachusetts. He coached at the University of Kansas.

> **Question:** What are the rules of the game?
>
> **Details:** Five people on a team; baskets score two points; use two baskets and one ball

> **Question:** How has basketball changed?
>
> **Details:** No longer use peach baskets or a soccer ball

Name _____

Follow your teacher's directions to complete this page.

1 **Topic:** The history of my favorite game _____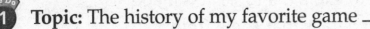

> **Question:**
>
> **Details:**

> **Question:**
>
> **Details:**

> **Question:**
>
> **Details:**

2 On a separate sheet of paper, fill in a graphic organizer like the one above. Write your ideas for a research report about a place you would like to visit. Think about questions you have about the topic. Then, research and write answers to the questions.

3 On a separate sheet of paper, prewrite a research report. You can also use what you have learned to make an old plan better.

Research Report

A **research report** uses facts to explain a topic. It is made up of several paragraphs with details that come from more than one source.

✏ Parts of a Research Report

- An introduction that tells or asks something interesting about the topic
- A body made up of one or more paragraphs
- A topic sentence and details for each paragraph
- A conclusion that sums up the report
- A list of sources you used

pencils

Introduction
Tells an interesting fact about the topic

→ Many sports have unusual histories. Basketball may be the only sport that was once a school assignment, though! Here's how it started.

Body
Has one or more paragraphs with topic sentences and details

→ **As the story goes**, basketball was invented in 1891 by a gym teacher named Dr. James Naismith. The athletes he worked with were bored being indoors all winter. Naismith was asked to find something to keep them out of trouble.

Luckily, he was reading about ancient Aztec and Mayan games. The old games gave him an idea. He nailed two peach baskets to a wall and tossed a soccer ball at them. Then he wrote down rules for a game with two baskets and a ball.

Other Words to Support Ideas
So that
Because of
As a result
For example
To sum up
For instance

Conclusion
Sums up the report

→ **Today**, basketball is not much like Dr. Naismith's game. However, the sport is now practiced around the world by millions of players.

Name _____

Follow your teacher's directions to complete the frame.

1 Have you ever wondered how people got the idea to start

playing _____? _____

_____

_____

_____

_____

_____

_____

_____

_____

_____

_____

_____

2 Think of a sport you would like to learn about. Look up facts in books, encyclopedias, magazines, and the Internet. Take notes on index cards. Then write a research report.

3 On a separate sheet of paper, use your prewriting plan to write a research report, or make a new plan to write about an activity you enjoy.

Prewriting

The **writing process** is a strategy that can help you write. It has five stages: prewriting, drafting, revising, editing, and publishing. **Prewriting** means planning before you write.

How to Prewrite

- First, think about your TAP. TAP stands for **T**ask, **A**udience, and **P**urpose.
- Plan by brainstorming ideas to write about. Some ways to brainstorm include making lists, freewriting, or looking through your journal.
- Choose one idea to write about. Circle it.
- Use a graphic organizer to decide which ideas to include in your writing.
- Gather details on your chosen idea, or topic.
- Put the details in order.

1 **Decide on your TAP.**

Task	Narrative
Audience	classmates
Purpose	tell a story

2 **Brainstorm ideas.**

- playing soccer
- (my new baby brother)
- my favorite book
- my first art class

3 **Gather information.**

New Baby Brother

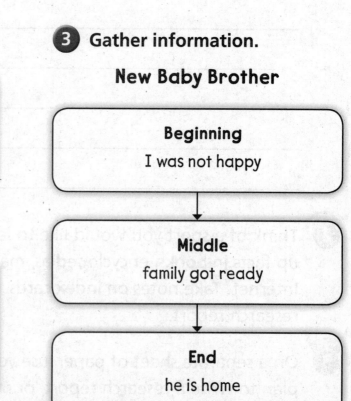

Beginning
I was not happy

↓

Middle
family got ready

↓

End
he is home

4 **Organize the information.** Choose the Graphic Organizer that works best with your **TAP.** Here are some examples:

Main Idea and Details Chart for Informational Writing

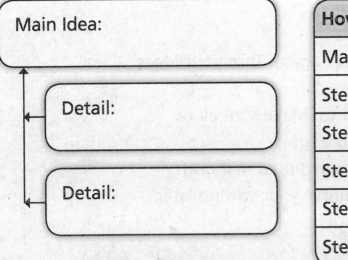

Main Idea:

Detail:

Detail:

Chart for How-to Paragraphs

How to _____
Materials:
Step 1
Step 2
Step 3
Step 4
Step 5

Venn Diagram to Compare and Contrast

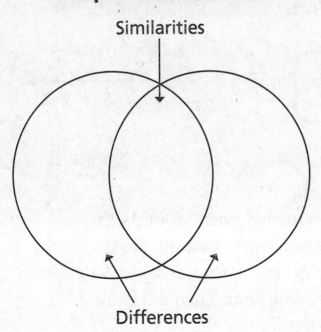

Similarities

Differences

5 W's Chart for Fictional Narrative

5 W's Chart
Who?
What?
When?
Where?
Why?

Drafting

Drafting is the second stage of the writing process. When you draft, you use your prewriting plan to guide what you write.

How to Draft

- Look at your graphic organizer again. Turn your ideas into full sentences.
- Add extra details if you need to. Make sure all of your sentences are on the same topic.
- This stage is sometimes called *writing a first draft*. You can make changes to improve your writing later.

New Baby Brother

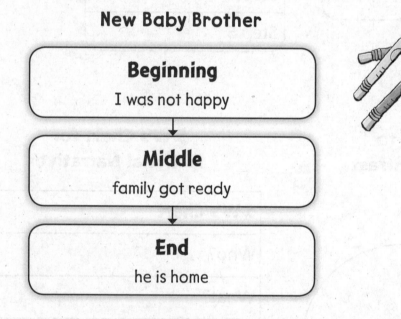

Beginning

I was not happy

↓

Middle

family got ready

↓

End

he is home

Draft

I know I should have been happy when I found out about my baby brother. I was not happy, though. No I was not! My family started to get ready for the baby. We painted his room and bought some stuff. Then the baby came home, and he was not so bad after all.

Topic: Raccoons

I. Northern raccoons

    a. Live in North and Central America

    b. Have thick, long gray fur

II. Crab-eating raccoons

    a. Live in Central and South America

    b. Have short, thin fur

Draft

There are two types of raccoons, northern raccoons and crab-eating raccoons. Northern raccoons live in North and Central America. They have thick, long gray fur. Crab-eating raccoons live in Central and South America. They have short, thin fur.

Opinion: Alice had a great adventure in Wonderland.

Reason: She changed sizes.

Reason: She could talk with animals.

Reason: She went to a party.

Draft

Alice had the most exciting adventure in Wonderland. First, she changed sizes. She got so small she couldn't reach the table! She found out she could talk to animals. Also, she went to a fun party.

Revising

Revising is the next stage in the writing process. **Revising** means improving your draft to make it clearer or more interesting. Don't worry about grammar or spelling mistakes yet.

Revising Checklist

- Is my writing focused? Is it supported by facts and details?
- Are my ideas clearly organized? Does the order make sense?
- Are there different types of sentences?
- Do I need to add or remove any details?

Ways to Revise

- Use editor's marks to show your changes. ⟶

Editor's Marks
≡ Make a capital.
∧ Insert.
˒ Delete.
⊙ Make a period.
∧ Insert a comma.
/ Make lowercase.

- Add words, sentences, or paragraphs.

I know I should have been happy when I found out about my baby brother. ∧ I never had a brother or a sister before.

- Cut information you don't need.

But I was not happy about it. ~~No I was not.~~ The day came and we got ready to bring him home.

- Replace information with something new or better.

But I was not happy about it. ~~No I was not!~~ The day

came and we got ready to bring him home. We

painted his room and bought some ~~stuff.~~ toys, diapers, and bottles.

- Move information so that it is in an order that makes sense.

(The day came and we got ready to bring him home.)

We painted his room and bought some ~~stuff.~~ toys, diapers, and bottles.

Here's how a revised draft might look:

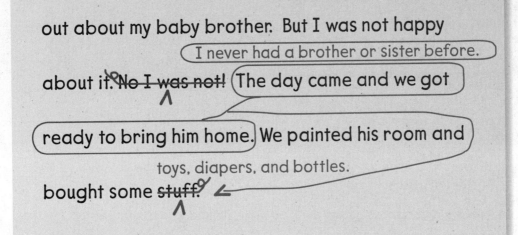

I know I should have been happy when I found

out about my baby brother. But I was not happy

(I never had a brother or sister before.)

about it. ~~No I was not!~~ (The day came and we got

ready to bring him home.) We painted his room and

bought some ~~stuff.~~ toys, diapers, and bottles.

Editing

Editing is the stage of the writing process that follows revision. During this stage, you find and fix mistakes.

✏ Editing

- Check for mistakes in punctuation, capitalization, spelling, and grammar.
- Make sure your paragraphs are indented.
- Use editor's marks to fix your writing.
- Use the spelling and grammar checker if you are working on a computer. Be sure to double-check your work for errors the checker won't catch.

Editor's Marks
≡ Make a capital.
∧ Insert.
⌿ Delete.
⊙ Make a period.
∧ Insert a comma.
/ Make lowercase.

Revised Draft

Carrie wanted a puppy. Instead, her mom and
dad said she would soon have a baby ~~siter~~ sister. Carrie
was not happy. Puppies were more ~~funner~~ fun than babies.
But on the day the ~~B~~aby came home, Carrie looked
at the pink bundle and fell in love.

Publishing

The last stage of the writing process is **publishing,** or sharing your writing with others. Before you publish, you can go back to any stage to improve your writing.

- Decide how you want to publish. You can share a written piece or give a presentation to your class.
- Type or write a clean copy of your piece.
- When you give a presentation, use note cards with the main ideas to guide you.

Jasper, My New Baby Brother

I know I should have been happy when I found out about my baby brother. I was not happy, though. I had never had a brother or sister before. We painted his room and bought some toys, diapers, and bottles. Dad let me help him put the crib together.

The day came, and we brought him home. Now that Jasper is home, I know he is a lot of fun. He smiles when I rock him, and he laughs and makes funny noises. I love my baby brother!

Evidence

Writing traits are the qualities found in all good writing. The six writing traits are evidence, organization, elaboration, purpose, development and conventions.

Evidence

- Do research to find a topic you are interested in.
- List facts, examples, and details to make sure your topic is a good one.
- Freewriting, listing, and discussing are good ways to make sure your topic is a good one with enough evidence.

Freewriting

I want to persuade the principal to let third-graders have recess again. I don't like sitting for such a long time. I get stiff and sleepy. Other students get grumpy. The principal is far away from my room. Maybe I can send a note?

Freewriting Tips
- Write whatever comes to mind.
- Don't worry about grammar or punctuation.
- Review your work and circle important ideas.

Listing

Topic: Making a Salad

Details:

-- good for you   (3)

-- good to eat   (2)

-- lettuce, tomato, cucumber

-- many types   (1)

Listing Tips
- Write a list of details about your topic.
- Choose the best details.
- Number them in the order you want to present them.

Informative Writing

- List what you already know about your topic, then do research.
- Good graphic organizers for evidence: web, note cards, timeline

Redwood trees are one of the oldest living things on earth.

-- can grow more than 350 feet tall

-- live for more than 1,000 years

Source: Kids Nature Magazine

Persuasive Writing

- Write your goal or opinion. Make a list of your thoughts and feelings.
- Research facts to support your goal or opinion.
- Good graphic organizers for ideas: idea-support map, column chart

Recycling		
reason: helps the environment **detail:** easy to do **detail:** creates less pollution	**reason:** protects animals and plants **detail:** animals can eat plastic and get sick	**reason:** saves money **detail:** good to use things again **detail:** bottles, cans, paper

Organization

Organization is the order in which you present your words and ideas. Different kinds of writing need different kinds of organization.

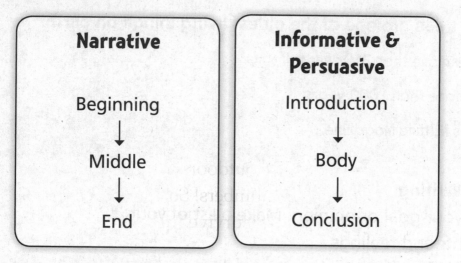

Narrative	Informative & Persuasive
Beginning	Introduction
↓	↓
Middle	Body
↓	↓
End	Conclusion

Narrative Writing

- A beginning that grabs readers' interest and introduces a problem
- A middle with events told in time order
- An ending that tells how the problem is solved

Beginning → Lynn's heart raced. She had lost her brother's bike! She thought she had chained it to the small oak tree near the pond, but the bike wasn't there. Maybe she had chained it to a different tree. She sprinted around the park. Where could it be? There

Middle → were too many trees, and the park was too big. Her head began to spin.

Finally, she decided to give up. She would have to tell Max that she could not find his bike. She walked toward the park's gate. Then she saw it. Max's shiny red bike was chained to the gate! Lynn

End → smiled and breathed a sigh of relief.

Informative Writing

- An introduction that grabs readers' attention
- A body that presents information or explains ideas in a logical order
- A conclusion that summarizes the information

Introduction →

Body →

Conclusion →

Do you think that a pet bird can escape and survive outside? Quaker Parrots are usually kept inside as pets, but a group of them escaped from a cargo plane at an airport almost 50 years ago. Now, flocks of them live outdoors in some states. They are even growing in numbers! So, the answer is YES! Some pet birds can survive in the wild.

Persuasive Writing

- An introduction, body, and conclusion
- Reasons presented in a logical order, such as least to most important

Reasons →

Swimming is the best sport. First, it makes you exercise every part of your body. Second, you can do it alone or with friends. Third, it helps with your breathing. Plus, moving in the water can feel like floating in space!

Purpose

Purpose is the reason a writer has for writing.

- Depending upon the purpose for writing, the audience will change.
- If your purpose for writing is to persuade or inform, you might use formal language. Formal words make your writing sound serious.
- If your purpose for writing is to tell a story or entertain, you might use an informal language. Informal words make your writing sound just like the way you talk.

Sample Informal Invitation

Hey Humberto,

    Can you and Elisa come to my birthday party on Saturday at 1:00? There will be cake, a clown, and gift bags.

                  Your friend,
                  Alicia

You can use informal language with people you know well.

Sample Formal Invitation

Dear Mrs. Best,

    You are invited to attend the graduation of my sister Tanya on November 4th at 5 PM at Clark Hall. Dinner will be served afterwards at 6:30 PM. Instead of gifts, Tanya has asked that you donate money to the dog shelter. Please RSVP.

                  Sincerely,
                  Natalia

You should use formal language with people you do not know well or have never met.

Elaboration

Elaboration, or the words and phrases a writer chooses, gives important information. It helps make characters, settings, actions, and events clear to readers.

> Aunt Anita and I make yummy blueberry pancakes every Saturday. First, we make a gooey batter from flour, baking powder, eggs, water, and salt. Then we mix in blueberries. Next, we heat a pan with butter and pour in the batter. We flip the pancakes once. Soon they are ready to eat.

As you revise, look for unclear or boring words to replace. Ask yourself:

- Do my **verbs** show exactly what is happening?
- Do the **nouns** create a clear picture?
- Are there **other words** I can add or change?

Not Exact:
The boy ate a big breakfast. Then he went to school.

Try replacing dull or unclear words with more descriptive words.

Exact:
Jamal gobbled up scrambled eggs, waffles, and bacon. Then he grabbed his green coat, ran to the bus, and went off to Northwood Elementary School.

Development

Good writers add clear details and descriptions to **develop** characters, settings, and events that seem real.

- Describe characters and settings clearly. Words and phrases such as *sunlight streaming through her window,* and *pans clanking and crashing* help readers feel as though they can see and hear what is happening.
- Use words like *soon, then, afterwards* to help readers understand the order of events.
- Make your writing interesting by writing different kinds of sentences. Vary how you begin sentences.

"Now everyone is stuck inside and no one will have any fun," <u>thought Lucy gloomily as she plopped down on her bed.</u> Today was the day of Lucy's school's Play Day that she had been looking forward to for a long time. <u>The rain was coming down so hard it looked like a waterfall streaming down her window.</u> Suddenly Lucy heard the sound of <u>pans clanking and crashing against each other.</u> <u>It wasn't long before grandmother called,</u> "Lucy, come on downstairs and let's bake cupcakes!"

The writer described what the character thought about the day's event.

This sentence helps readers understand what the weather was like and why the character felt gloomy.

This phrase helps readers to hear the noise the character heard.

These words help readers understand what the character will be doing next.

Use a variety of sentence beginnings.

Too Many Sentences Beginning the Same Way

Ron grabbed his backpack. He put his lucky baseball mitt inside. He checked his backpack one last time. He called to his mother, "I'm ready for the game!"

Variety of Sentence Beginnings

Ron grabbed his backpack. <u>Then</u> he put his lucky baseball mitt inside. <u>After checking his backpack one last time</u>, he called to his mother, "I'm ready for the game!"

Create different sentence lengths.

Too Many Sentences of the Same Length

Jawara called his sister. He asked to borrow her computer. He had a project to do. He went to her room. He turned the computer on. He waited for it to start up. He said, "This computer is taking forever."

Varied Lengths

Jawara called his sister. He asked to borrow her computer because he had a project to do. When he got to her room, he turned the computer on. After waiting a few minutes for it to start up, he thought, "This computer is taking forever."

Connect ideas from sentence to sentence in the right order.

Unconnected ideas

Carnivals have been entertaining people for a long time. We have never had one in our city. It had a lot of games and food and rides. I won a stuffed giraffe! There was a contest to guess how many pennies were in a jar.

Connected ideas

Carnivals have been entertaining people for a long time, but we have never had one in our city before. It had a lot of games, food, and rides. There was a contest to guess how many pennies were in a jar, and I won a stuffed giraffe!

Conventions

Conventions are rules for grammar, spelling, punctuation, and capitalization. One way to make sure you are following the rules when you write or edit is to have an editing checklist.

Sample Editing Checklist

Punctuation

___ Did I use correct end punctuation in my sentences?

___ Did I use commas correctly in compound sentences?

___ Did I use quotation marks correctly?

Capitalization

___ Did I start every sentence with a capital letter?

___ Did I capitalize proper nouns?

Spelling

___ Did I spell all of my words correctly?

Grammar

___ Did my sentences have correct subject-verb agreement?

___ Did I avoid sentence fragments?

Common Errors

Sentence Fragments

A sentence should have both a subject and a verb.

Wrong Way	Right Way
A leaf from a tree.	The leaf fell from the tree.
Because autumn is coming.	I feel happy because autumn is coming.
Piles of leaves on the ground to jump in.	Soon, there will be piles of leaves on the ground to jump in.

Common and Proper Nouns

Most nouns are **common nouns**. These are general people, places, or things, and are not capitalized. A **proper noun** names a specific person, place, or thing. Proper nouns are always capitalized.

Wrong Way	Right Way
I talked to the Teacher about my vacation.	I talked to the teacher about my vacation.
Then mrs. morris told me about her trip to mexico.	Then Mrs. Morris told me about her trip to Mexico.

Subject-Verb Agreement

Make sure the subject and verb of your sentence agree.

Wrong Way	Right Way
Mario eat pizza on Saturdays.	Mario eats pizza on Saturdays.
Terri and Lucia runs to the corner and back every day.	Terri and Lucia run to the corner and back every day.

Correct use of commas in sentences

When you list three or more items in a sentence, it is called a **series**. Put commas between items in a series. Use a comma to combine two sentences into one compound sentence.

Wrong Way	Right Way
My new hat was green red and blue.	My new hat was green, red, and blue.
Annie came for a visit, I wasn't home.	Annie came for a visit, but I wasn't home.

Writing Workshop

During a **writing workshop**, writers read each other's work. Then they ask questions and suggest changes to improve each other's writing.

How a Writing Workshop Works

- Listen to your classmates' questions and suggestions.
- Make changes if their ideas make sense to you.
- Listen carefully as your classmates read their work.
- Tell classmates what you liked about their work.
- Ask thoughtful questions and make useful comments.

Maybe you could just say, "I couldn't see the letters very well."

Do you need this sentence?

This is a great detail! It makes me feel like I'm there.

This part made me laugh.

I remember when I got glasses for the first time. I was having trouble seeing the board in school, so my mom took me to see Dr. Jett.

Dr. Jett gave me some tests. He was nice! He told me to look at some letters and tell him what they were. Like if it was a V or a W. I couldn't see them very well. He told Mom that I needed glasses. So we went to the glasses store. I tried on 23 pairs before I found one I liked.

We bought the glasses. They cost $99.99, plus tax. That was about $50 for each eye! Mom said she was glad I didn't have three eyes, because then my glasses would cost too much!

Tips for a Workshop

Sharing your writing will help you improve your work and find mistakes you did not see. Helping others with their writing also helps you find ways to fix your own writing.

During Prewriting

Working with others can help you...

- brainstorm topics to write about.
- find information about your topic.

As You Review Your First Draft

Working with others can tell you...

- what they liked.
- what parts they have questions about.

As You Revise

Working with others can tell you if...

- the beginning gets their interest.
- the middle part sticks to the topic.
- the ending is strong.

As You Edit and Proofread

Working with others can help you...

- check your capitalization.
- check your punctuation.
- check your spelling.

Using the Internet

The Internet is a great place to find information. Once you have a topic to research, you can search websites to answer your questions.

- A search engine will help you find websites about your topic. If you are not sure whether a particular website is a good source, ask your teacher.
- Many encyclopedias, dictionaries, magazines, and newspapers can be found online.
- Be sure to record your sources. When you take notes, write down the address, or the URL, of the website. Look for the author and the date.

Parts of a Website

URL	Address http://www.---.org
Website title	THE FIRST CARS
Author's name	ABOUT US by Edmund Johns
Date published	9/20/12

File   Edit   View   Favorites   Tools   Help

LINKS

NEWS

Can you imagine life when the only way to get around was by horse-drawn car? The first cars as we know them were created in the 1800s. Inventors figured out how to create an engine that ran by heating coal. Soon after that, cars were created that ran on gas. The first gas powered car built in America was in 1893.

Print, Highlight, and Reword

If you find a website you like, you can highlight the important parts in another color. When you write your report, put the information in your own words.

Flamingos

by Stacy Fiore

If you have seen a flamingo, you know it is a tall pink bird. That is just one kind of flamingo, though. There are actually five kinds of flamingos! They all have long necks and long legs, but not all are pink. Some flamingos are black, red, or yellow.

Writing for the Web

There are many ways to use technology to write. One way is to write for the web.

✎ E-mail

You can send e-mail to a friend or family member. You can also use e-mail for business, which requires more formal language. An e-mail is a lot like a letter. You can write an e-mail to connect with anyone around the world who has an e-mail address.

Heading
Includes the recipient's **e-mail address** and a **subject line**

Beginning
Tells why you are writing

Middle
Tells what happened

End
Wraps up the message

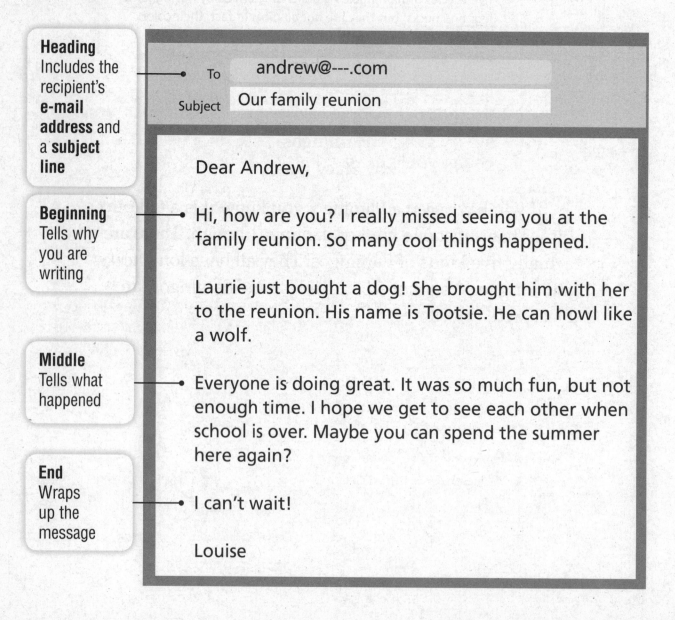

To andrew@---.com

Subject Our family reunion

Dear Andrew,

Hi, how are you? I really missed seeing you at the family reunion. So many cool things happened.

Laurie just bought a dog! She brought him with her to the reunion. His name is Tootsie. He can howl like a wolf.

Everyone is doing great. It was so much fun, but not enough time. I hope we get to see each other when school is over. Maybe you can spend the summer here again?

I can't wait!

Louise

Blog Post

Blog is short for "weblog." It is a journal that you keep on the Internet so that other people can read and comment. One way to use a blog is to share news about friends, family, or yourself. Blogs can also be essays or include opinions.

URL ────────

Blog Name ────────

Post Title ────────

Byline
Tells who wrote the post and when it was published

Body
Tells what happens or gives thoughts and opinions

Comments
Left by readers

File   Edit   View   Favorites   Tools   Help

Address http://www.---.com/blog

Lindsey Smart's Solar Energy Blog

Cars can be solar, too!

by Lindsey on December 1, 2012 at 4:17pm

You might have heard of many uses for solar energy. But do you know that you can use solar energy to power your car?

Solar cells work with car engines to make them run longer. Using solar power will help reduce the pollution created by cars and other vehicles.

Some countries are using solar powered cars already. I hope in the future we can all use solar power to run our cars, trucks, buses, trains, and even motorcycles. What do you think?

Comments

Marcy C:
I had no idea that solar cars were already being used in other places! Is there anywhere my family can get one?

Doing Research

The best way to support your ideas in persuasive or informative writing is to use facts and details. The best way to find facts and details is to do research. Remember to record your sources so that you can cite them later.

Sources of Information

- Books
- Encyclopedias
- Magazines
- Newspapers
- Digital Audio, CDs, DVDs
- The Internet
- Television and Videos
- Interviews

Evaluating Sources

Some sources are more reliable than others. How can you tell which sources are good? When looking at a new source, ask yourself these questions:

☐ Is the source published by experts in that field?

☐ If it is a website, can you trust it? (If you are not sure, then you can ask your teacher. Sites that end in *.edu*, *.org*, or *.gov* are usually websites you can trust.)

☐ Is the source recent and up to date?

☐ Is the information useful and complete?

Finding Information

A library is organized to help you find information. The books in a library are divided into three main sections: Fiction, Nonfiction, and Reference Books.

- **Fiction** books include stories and novels. These books are arranged by the authors' last names.
- **Nonfiction** (factual) books are arranged by call numbers, according to the Dewey decimal system.
- **Reference** books such as encyclopedias, atlases, and dictionaries are kept in a special section of the library.

Other reference material may include:

- **Magazines** and **Newspapers**. These may be found in the periodicals area.
- **Computer labs**. Computers with connection to the Internet may be at your library.
- **Media Section**. DVDs, CDs, videos, and computer software may be found in the Media Section.

Tips: How to Use the Dewey Decimal System

- A book numbered **386** comes before a book numbered **714**
- One labeled **973A** comes before one labeled **973B**.
- Some call numbers have decimals, like **973.19** or **973.22**. Ask your librarian if you need help finding these books.

Notetaking

You will find a lot of information when you research. One way to keep track of it and stay organized is to take notes.

✏️ Note Cards

You can take notes on your research in two ways.

1. You can write a main idea or a research question at the top of the card. Then write details or the answer to your research question below. At the bottom, be sure to include your source.

Main Idea	● Biography about Amelia Earhart
Details	● -- First woman to fly solo across Atlantic Ocean! -- Flew in 1932 from Canada to Ireland -- She wanted to prove that a woman could do it
Source	● Source: Jerome, Kate Boehm. <u>Who Was Amelia Earhart?</u> New York: Grosset & Dunlap, 2002. p. 37

2. You can write your research question at the top and then include a direct quote from the source. Include your source at the bottom.

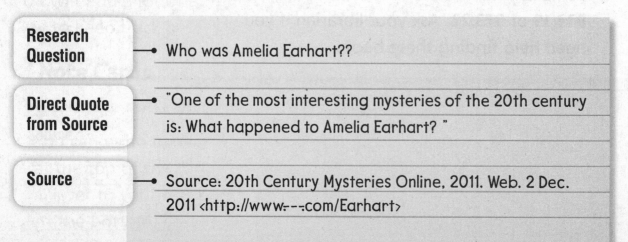

Research Question	● Who was Amelia Earhart??
Direct Quote from Source	● "One of the most interesting mysteries of the 20th century is: What happened to Amelia Earhart? "
Source	● Source: 20th Century Mysteries Online, 2011. Web. 2 Dec. 2011 <http://www.---.com/Earhart>

Writing to Learn

Think-Aloud on Paper

- As you read, list ideas you want to remember.
- Use diagrams, drawings, or graphic organizers to show how ideas connect.
- As you read, write questions in a journal or log. Later, research the answers to your questions, or ask your teacher for help.

Learning Logs

- A learning log is a place for you to comment on, ask questions about, or make connections to your reading.
- In the left column, **Note-Taking,** write the exact words you read.
- In the right column, **Note-Making,** write thoughts and questions about the notes in the left column.

Learning Log: "Amelia Disappears! "	
Note-Taking	Note-Making
"In June 1937, she left Miami, Florida, on an around-the-world flight attempt."	Was she the first person to try to fly around the world?
" ...she flew with copilot Lieutenant Commander Noonan"	I wonder how she picked him as her copilot.
"On July 2, the plane disappeared near Howland Island in the South Pacific."	How far is the South Pacific from Miami, where she began her flight attempt?

Writing to a Prompt

A prompt is a writing assignment. Sometimes teachers give timed writing assignments for class exercises or tests.

Writing to a Prompt

- Read the prompt carefully.
- Note whether it asks you to give information, express opinions, or persuade someone.
- Plan your writing before you begin to draft.
- Restate the key parts of the prompt in your topic sentence.
- If you have a time limit, then plan your time carefully.

Prompt:

Think about how to take care of a plant. Now write a paragraph describing things a plant needs to grow.

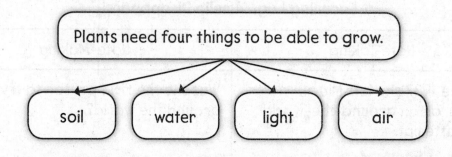

Draft

Plants need four things to be able to grow. These four things are soil, light, water, and air. Plants get nutrients from the soil to help them grow. Also, they use light from the sun for energy. The plants cannot live on just light. They put the sunlight, water, and gases from the air together to make oxygen and sugar. The plants use the sugar to grow. We use the oxygen to breathe!

Prompts

Prompts often ask for different kinds of writing. Here is an example of a narrative prompt:

> Everyone has a favorite pastime. Think about how you like to spend your free time. Now write a story about a day you spent enjoying your favorite pastime.

Here are some other types of written prompts:

Fictional Narrative	Persuasive Writing
These prompts ask you to "tell a story."	These prompts ask you to "convince" or "persuade."
Informative Writing	**Response to Literature**
These prompts ask you to "tell or explain why."	These prompts ask you to answer questions about a piece you read.

Here is an example of a persuasive prompt:

> Many people have a favorite type of music. Think about the music you like. Now write a letter persuading a friend that the type of music you enjoy is the best.

Checklists and Rubrics

A **rubric** is a chart that helps you when you write and revise. Score 6 tells you what to aim for in your writing.

	• Focus • Support	• Organization
Score 6	My writing is focused and supported by facts or details.	My writing has an introduction and conclusion. Ideas are clearly organized.
Score 5	My writing is mostly focused and supported by facts or details.	My writing has an introduction and a conclusion. Ideas are mostly organized.
Score 4	My writing is mostly focused and supported by some facts or details.	My writing has an introduction and a conclusion. Most ideas are organized.
Score 3	Some of my writing is focused and supported by some facts or details.	My writing has an introduction or a conclusion but might be missing one. Some ideas are organized.
Score 2	My writing is not focused and is supported by few facts or details.	My writing might not have an introduction or a conclusion. Few ideas are organized.
Score 1	My writing is not focused or supported by facts or details.	My writing is missing an introduction and a conclusion. Few or no ideas are organized.

Elaboration Purpose	Conventions Development • Evidence
My purpose is strong. My writing grabs the readers' interest. Words strongly support purpose.	My writing has no errors in spelling, grammar, capitalization, or punctuation. Writing includes descriptions, details, and/or reasons.
My purpose is strong throughout. Writing is interesting to readers. Word choice is appropriate for my purpose.	My writing has few errors in spelling, grammar, capitalization, or punctuation. Writing includes many descriptions, details, and reasons.
My purpose is explained at the beginning or end. Writing mostly holds readers' interest. Many word choices are appropriate.	My writing has some errors in spelling, grammar, capitalization, or punctuation. Writing includes a few examples of descriptions, details, and reasons.
My purpose is somewhat clear. Writing is interesting but needs more description. Many word choices are good.	My writing has some errors in spelling, grammar, capitalization, or punctuation. Writing includes a few examples of description, details, and reasons.
My purpose is unclear. Writing holds reader's interest in places. Some word choices are good.	My writing has many errors in spelling, grammar, capitalization, or punctuation. There is little variety of sentences. Some sentences are incomplete.
My purpose is not clear. Writing isn't very interesting to read.	My writing has many errors in spelling, grammar, capitalization, or punctuation. There is no variety of sentences. Sentences are incomplete.

Summary

A **summary** tells the reader about the plot and characters in a book or story.

✎ Parts of a Summary

- An introduction that tells the reader the name of the book and its author
- Body paragraphs that describe the main events in the plot
- A conclusion that tells the end of the story

pencils

Introduction
Gives the main idea of the book

Body
Tells about the characters and plot

Stuart Little by E.B. White

The book *Stuart Little* by E.B. White is about a mouse named Stuart and his adventures in a really big city. Stuart gets into a lot of problems, but he has good friends who help him.

Stuart Little was born into a family of humans. However, Stuart is a mouse! At first, it was weird for the family to be living with a mouse. After a while, the whole family loved Stuart because he was so nice. The Littles quickly learned what a good son Stuart was. When Mrs. Little dropped her ring down the sink, Stuart helped her. Stuart was so small that he was able to go right down the drain to get the ring!

Stuart also lived with a cat named Snowball. While the whole family loved Stuart, Snowball did not like him. Snowball was jealous of Stuart and all the attention he got from the rest of the family.

Other Transitions
Second
After that
Soon
Meanwhile
Eventually
Finally
Later

Snowball started being mean to Stuart. One day, Snowball got Stuart trapped in the window.

Stuart had many more adventures and got into trouble a lot. He was very curious. Once, he got lost in Central Park and got swept out to sea. A bird named Margalo saved him. Margalo took Stuart back to his home. Then Stuart and Margalo became very good friends.

One day, Stuart learned that some of the neighborhood cats were planning to eat Margalo. Stuart told his friend, and Margalo decided to fly away for good. Stuart became really sad after that. He missed his good friend a lot.

Conclusion
Describes the end of the book

Soon after, Stuart Little decided to go look for Margalo. Stuart got a toy car that ran on gas and headed north. The book ends with Stuart leaving to find his friend and have more exciting adventures.

Note how the author of this piece:

- Introduced the book by telling its title, author, and main character.

The book *Stuart Little* by E.B. White is about a mouse named Stuart and his adventures in a really big city.

- Told the events of the story in time order.

Cause and Effect

The **cause-and-effect essay** describes how or why something happens. The cause is an event or action. This leads to an effect, or a result.

Parts of a Cause-and-Effect Essay

- An **introduction** that explains the main cause and effect
- Paragraphs with **examples** of cause and effect
- A **conclusion** that summarizes the main idea

How Prospect Park Was Saved

> An action happens because of a **cause**

Last month Prospect Park reopened because a group of people decided to fix it. A year ago, the park was a mess. For years, no one had taken care of it. Once it had been a place where people came to have fun. Now the park was empty.

> **Effect** What happens as a result of the cause

The ball fields could not be used because weeds grew everywhere. The team benches had fallen down. Garbage covered the outfield, and the grass had died.

The gardens had once been filled with flowers. But no one had taken care of them for years. Now they were filled with dead plants and weeds.

That was not all. The fence around the dog run had fallen down, so no dogs could exercise there. Not even the benches could be used because they were broken.

> **Cause**

In March of last year, however, a few people decided to do something about Prospect Park. They spoke up at a town meeting, and Mayor Griggs set up a

> **Effect**

committee to start to fix the park.

These paragraphs offer more examples of cause and effect.

One group of people raised money. They convinced hardware stores to give materials for building, and many people gave money, too.

Another group got volunteers to work at the park each weekend. Soon the ball fields were better than ever. People made new gardens, benches, and even barbecue pits!

Finally, dog owners volunteered time to build a new dog run. They fixed fences and gates and put in water bowls. Soon it was a place that dogs would love.

The committee worked long and hard for almost a year. In the end, their work paid off. Last month, over a thousand people came to the park's grand re-opening.

Since then, the action in the park has not stopped. Little league and adult baseball teams play every day. Volunteers keep the gardens beautiful. The lawns are covered with soft, wonderful-smelling grass. Best of all, the dogs play whenever they want in the new dog run.

Conclusion

All this happened because a few people cared about making Prospect Park a great place for everyone.

Note how the writer of this piece:

- Began the essay by stating the main cause and effect.
  Another way the writer could have introduced the essay is to ask a question:
  How did people save Prospect Park?

- Went on to describe a situation.

- Continued by telling what was done to change that situation.

- Used a conclusion that summed up what was done.

Problem/Solution

In a **problem-solution essay,** the writer presents a difficult situation, or problem. Then the writer explains a solution to the problem.

Parts of a Problem-Solution Essay

- An introduction that describes the problem
- Possible solutions that might solve the problem
- A conclusion that describes how the problem was solved

pencils

Too Many Cats!

Introduction
Begins the story and gives background to the problem

Last summer my cat Lucy got sick. She stayed under the porch for days and would not come out. We tried everything to get her to come inside. We called her. We left food out for her. Nothing seemed to work, and Lucy stayed under the porch. Finally, my father decided to crawl under the porch to get Lucy. When he came back out, he was carrying several tiny kittens! Lucy wasn't sick after all. She was under the porch taking care of her new kittens!

My father brought Lucy and her kittens inside. We put them all in a box in the closet. There were six in all. The kittens were so small they couldn't even open their eyes. Lucy was a good mother. She stayed with them day and night.

Other Transitions
Last summer
Finally
A few days later
One by one
Then
After a couple weeks

Body
Describes the difficult situation or problem

A few days later, my mother told me that we could not keep all the kittens. "We already have two dogs and a cat," she said. "We just don't have room for a bunch of kittens."

This paragraph explores ways to solve the problem.

Here the author describes her solution to the problem.

Conclusion Describes what happened when she tried her solution

I was sad, but I knew she was right. Caring for six kittens is a lot of work. My mother asked me what I wanted to do about the kittens. We could bring them all down to the animal shelter. Or we could try to find good homes for them ourselves.

We decided to find homes for the kittens. That way we could make sure each kitten found a good family to live with. I made signs about the kittens. The signs had pictures of the kittens and our phone number. Then we put up the signs in places like the grocery store and the post office.

After a few days, we started to get phone calls about the kittens. Different people came by to see the kittens. One by one each kitten found a new home. We made sure each kitten was going to nice people. Finally, there was one kitten left. He was small and quiet. After a couple of weeks, no one came to look at the last kitten. Then one day my father said to me, "Let's keep this one." I was so happy! We got a new kitten!

Note how the author of this piece:

- Introduced the problem to the reader by telling a story.

- Used transition words and phrases to move the story along.
  A few days later, my mother told me that we could not keep all the kittens.

- Used dialogue to describe the problem and make the story sound realistic.
  "We already have two dogs and a cat," she said. "We just don't have room for a bunch of kittens."

Writing for Science

An **observation report** uses narrative to describe events during scientific observation. These observations can help explain how things work.

Parts of an Observation Report

- A purpose that explains the reasons for the study
- Observations that describe what was seen
- A conclusion that describes what was learned

A Tale of Tadpoles

Purpose
Introduces the study and describes why it was performed

Purpose:
Frogs begin life as tadpoles. Then they slowly turn into frogs. We observed these changes in class.

Observations
Describe different events that occurred during the study

Observations:
MAY 9: Our tadpoles arrived in class. They will stay in an aquarium. They are about two weeks old.
MAY 16: Some of the tadpoles have grown very small legs, but others have not.
MAY 23: All of the tadpoles now have at least small legs. Some tadpoles have much larger legs.
MAY 30: Several of the tadpoles have lost their tails. Some are even climbing out of the water.
JUNE 6: Nearly all of the tadpoles have lost their tails. They all look like little frogs now.

Conclusion
Reviews the study and describes what was learned

Conclusion:
Tadpoles take several weeks to transform into frogs. They lose their tails and grow legs. After about six weeks of growing, tadpoles become frogs.

Writing for Math

A **story problem** uses math to answer a question. The parts of the equation are found within the story itself.

✎ Parts of a Story Problem

- A problem that needs to be solved
- A section that clearly describes the math equations
- A solution to the problem

Beginning
Introduces the problem to the reader

A Pumpkin Problem

The Problem: Abrams' Farm is selling pumpkins for Halloween. Small pumpkins sell for $3 each. Medium-sized pumpkins are $6 and large pumpkins are $10 each. On Saturday, Abrams' Farm sold five small pumpkins, three medium pumpkins, and eight large pumpkins. How much money did Abrams' Farm make from pumpkins on Saturday?

This paragraph clearly explains the operation needed to solve the problem.

Operation: First, identify how many pumpkins were sold at each price. Then multiply the number of pumpkins sold by the price for each pumpkin. Finally, add them together to get the total amount.

This section turns the word problem into simple math equations.

5 small pumpkins at $3 each   = 5 x 3 = $15
3 medium pumpkins at $6 each = 3 x 6 = $18
8 large pumpkins at $10 each   = 8 x 10 = $80
                                                    Total   = $113

Solution
Gives the solution to the problem

Solution: Abrams' Farm sold a total of $113 worth of pumpkins on Saturday.

How-to Essay

A **how-to essay** describes how to do something. This type of essay has very clear step-by-step directions to help the reader complete the project.

Parts of a How-to Essay

- An introduction that gets the reader interested
- A list of supplies needed to complete the project
- Clear directions on how to complete the project
- A conclusion that wraps up the directions

pencils

How to Make Casts of Animal Tracks

Introduction
Gets readers interested in the project

Some animals are very hard to see. Animals like raccoons and coyotes usually only come out at night when people are asleep. Although we rarely get to see these animals, they sometimes leave behind tracks, or paw prints. These tracks can tell us a lot about animals. They can tell us which animals live near us. Tracks can also tell us about the way animals behave.

You can collect animal tracks by making plaster casts. This project can be done just about anywhere you might find animals. Here is a list of the supplies you will need.

Other Transitions
First
Also
Next
Then
After
Last
Once

A list of supplies tells readers what they will need to complete the project.

1. A tin can with both ends cut off
2. Plaster of Paris (to make the cast)
3. An animal track!
4. A wildlife field guide

Body
Guides
readers
through the
project step
by step

First, locate an animal track in your backyard or on a hiking trail. This track should have obvious parts, such as toes, claws, and a footpad.

Next, remove any debris from the track, such as leaves or sticks. Then place the tin can around the track. Press the can into the soil about 1-inch deep.

After you press the can into the soil, stir ½ cup of Plaster of Paris with water until the mixture is thick like pancake batter. Pour the mixture into the can and cover the track. There should be about 1 inch of plaster in the bottom of the can. Let the plaster dry for at least one hour before removing the can from the ground. Then let the plaster cast dry for another 24 hours before removing it from the can.

Conclusion
Tells readers
what they
can do after
they have
completed the
project

Once you remove the cast, use your field guide to help you identify what animal made the track.

Note how the author of this piece:

- Introduced the project by getting the reader interested in the subject.

  Other ways she could have introduced the project are to ask a question or state a fact.

  Have you ever wanted to learn about animals that are hard to see?

  Scientists use animal tracks to learn about many kinds of animals.

- Told the reader what to do after completing the project.

  Once you remove the cast from the can, use your field guide to help you identify what animal made the track.

Explanation

An **explanation** essay is used to describe or inform. In this example, the author explains where she would visit if she had the chance.

Parts of an Explanation

- An introduction that offers a main idea
- A body that has paragraphs to support the main idea
- A conclusion that reviews the main idea and supporting paragraphs

Introduction
Tells the main idea and explains why the reader might find it interesting

My Visit to Greece

If I could go anywhere in the world, I would like to visit the country of Greece. This country has lots of great history and culture. Greece also has many beaches and islands to visit. Most of all, I would like to visit because both of my grandparents are from Greece.

Greece is a country with a lot of culture and history. Many of the great myths come from Greece. I like to read Greek myths, and visiting the places I have read about would be exciting. A long time ago, most Greeks believed in many gods. The Greeks built temples and other buildings for these gods. Many of these temples are still standing, and you can visit them today. I would visit the Temple of Apollo, the god of the sun. I would also visit the Parthenon, which is located in Athens. The Parthenon was built to honor Athena, the goddess of wisdom. Athens is named after her, too.

Body
Supports the main idea of the essay with examples and facts

Supporting Ideas
history
culture
beaches
islands
grandparents
adventure
family

Greece is located on the Mediterranean Sea, so the weather is terrific all year round. One of my favorite parts of Greece would be visiting the beaches and the many small villages around the countryside.

Each supporting paragraph has a topic sentence that explains the main idea of the paragraph.

Most of all, I would like to visit Greece because my grandmother and grandfather are from there. Both of my grandparents were born in Athens in 1940. They got married in 1960 and then moved to the United States. They have gone back to visit friends and family many times. My parents have gone with them, too. When they got back home last time they told me a lot of funny stories about our family in Greece. I would really like to meet my Greek cousins. My grandmother says I can go with them to Greece next summer. I can't wait!

Conclusion Reviews the main ideas of the essay and explains why the subject is interesting

Greece is a country full of history. The country has done a terrific job preserving this history for the world to come see. My own family history is part of Greece, too. Because of this, Greece is the one place in the world I would like to visit.

Note how the author of this piece:

- Used the first paragraph to introduce the main idea and supporting details.

- Included topic sentences that introduced the main idea of each paragraph.
  Most of all I would like to visit Greece because my grandmother and grandfather are from there.

- Reviewed the main idea and supporting details in the conclusion.

Research Report

In a **research report**, the author informs the reader about a topic. The author first researches the topic and then uses these facts to create an essay.

Parts of a Research Report

- An introduction that tells the reader something interesting about the topic
- A body that gives details and facts to support the main idea
- A conclusion that reviews the main ideas about the topic

Introduction
Tells about the subject and explains why the author finds it interesting

Body
Has paragraphs that support the author's main ideas

Salamanders!

Salamanders are very interesting animals. They come in all different sizes and colors and can be found just about anywhere. You can even find salamanders in your backyard!

Salamanders have a fascinating lifecycle. Like frogs, salamanders are amphibians. Some salamanders lay their eggs in lakes or ponds. When the eggs hatch, the little salamanders have gills to help them breathe under water. Over a few weeks, salamanders grow and change. They lose their gills and breathe air. Then they leave the pond and walk on land. Adult salamanders live under rotten logs, leaves, or rocks in wet areas.

Many salamanders in North America do not have lungs. These salamanders can breathe right through their skin! Because of this, salamanders have to keep their skin moist. This is why salamanders like to live in wet or muddy places. If you ever catch a salamander, make sure your hands are wet. Handling a salamander with dry hands can hurt their wet skin.

These paragraphs continue to support the author's main idea. They also offer many interesting facts about salamanders.

There are almost 500 different species of salamanders found around the world. About 100 different kinds of salamanders live in the United States. The Great Smoky Mountains National Park is known as the "Salamander Capital of the World." This is because so many different kinds of salamanders live in the park.

The largest salamander in the United States is called the hellbender. It can grow up to two feet long! These salamanders are very hard to find because they only come out at night. Also, hellbenders live in large rivers and spend most of their time hiding under rocks. The hellbender is big, but it is not the largest salamander in the world. The Chinese giant salamander can grow as large as six feet long! Luckily these giant creatures are only found in Asia.

Conclusion Reviews the main idea and supporting paragraphs

Salamanders are very cool animals. There are many different kinds of salamanders, too. These animals can be found just about anywhere. Next time you are out hiking, turn over some rotten logs. You'll never know what you might find hiding there!

Note how the writer of this piece:

- Introduced the topic of the essay in the first paragraph.

  Another way the writer could have introduced the topic is to ask a question to grab the reader's attention.

  Which animal can be many shapes and sizes and live in your own backyard? Salamanders are very interesting animals.

- Included supporting paragraphs with interesting facts

Graphs, Diagrams, and Charts

Graphs, diagrams, and charts help make ideas clear. You can use them in your informative writing, such as a research report.

A **title** tells the reader what the diagram is about.

A **flow chart** is a type of diagram that shows how things change over time or the different steps in a process.

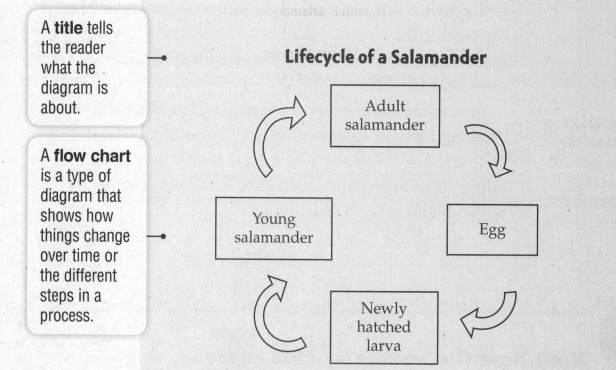

Lifecycle of a Salamander

Adult salamander → Egg → Newly hatched larva → Young salamander → Adult salamander

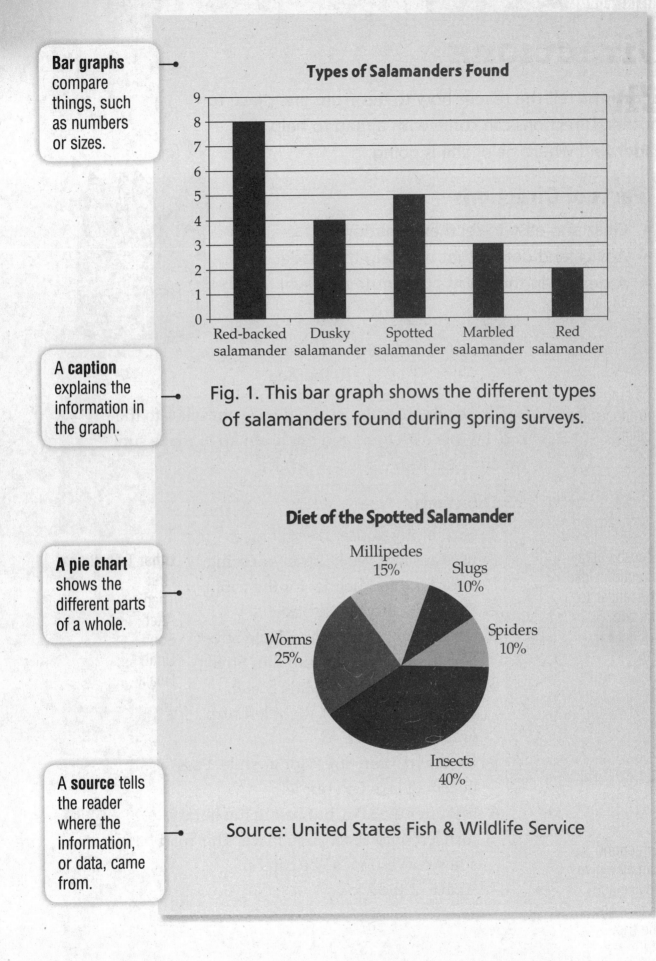

Bar graphs compare things, such as numbers or sizes.

Types of Salamanders Found

A **caption** explains the information in the graph.

Fig. 1. This bar graph shows the different types of salamanders found during spring surveys.

A pie chart shows the different parts of a whole.

Diet of the Spotted Salamander

Millipedes 15%
Slugs 10%
Spiders 10%
Worms 25%
Insects 40%

A **source** tells the reader where the information, or data, came from.

Source: United States Fish & Wildlife Service

Directions

Directions tell the reader how to get from one place to another. Directions can come with a map to help the reader find where he or she is going.

Parts of Directions

- Clear and easy-to-read explanations
- Advice and details that will help the reader
- A clear map that shows the route of travel

To the Zoo!

> The author introduces the activity.

Today, my friends and I will ride our bikes to the zoo. I wrote directions and made a map to make sure we don't get lost.

Directions

> Step-by-step directions lead the reader to the zoo.

1. Start at my house. We will meet here at 11am. Make sure you bring your bike and helmet for the trip!
2. Turn left onto Maple Street.
3. Go about one block on Maple Street and then turn right onto Elm Street.
4. Then, turn left onto Main Street. This is going to be a slight left turn onto Main Street.
5. Go down Main Street for a while. Pass the small lake on your left.
6. Just after the lake, but before the library, turn left onto Peach Tree Place. This road has a few curves in it so be careful!

> Directions can also give advice and details about the trip.

7. Arrive at the zoo!

Other Transitions
First
Then
After
Soon
Until
Finally

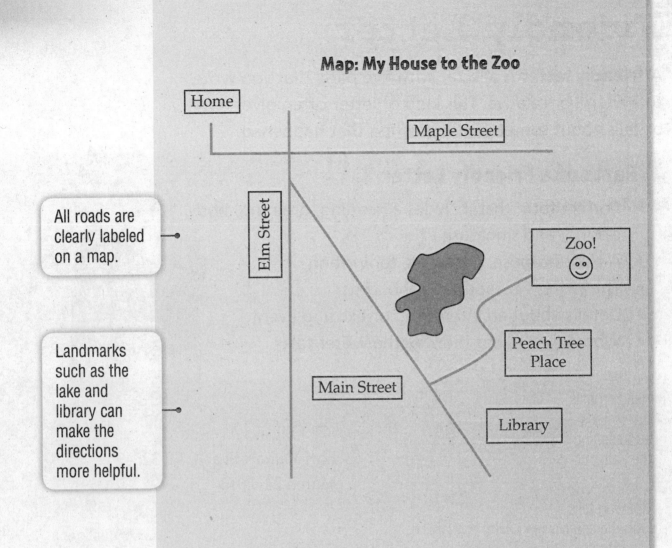

Map: My House to the Zoo

Home

Maple Street

Elm Street

Zoo!
:)

Peach Tree Place

Main Street

Library

All roads are clearly labeled on a map.

Landmarks such as the lake and library can make the directions more helpful.

Note how the author of this piece:

- Used turn-by-turn directions to describe the route to the destination.

- Created a simple map to go with the clear directions.

- Provided advice and details about landmarks along the route that could help the reader find the destination.

Friendly Letter

A **friendly letter** is a letter with five parts that you write to a friend or relative. This kind of letter often gives news or tells about something interesting that happened.

Parts of a Friendly Letter

- Correct form that includes a heading, greeting, body, closing, and signature
- A clear purpose, or reason, for writing
- The writer's feelings and thoughts
- Details about an interesting or exciting event
- Words that sound the way the writer talks

pencils

Heading tells the writer's address and the date	6733 Eighth Avenue Fort Walton Beach, FL 32549 March 24, 2013
Greeting tells who the letter is written to	Dear Kathleen,

Wait until you hear about my weekend! Yesterday, I went on the best roller coaster. My dad rode with me. First, we went way up in the sky. Then, we dropped almost straight down. I felt like my stomach jumped into my throat! Everyone screamed, even my dad. After that, the coaster made two loops. I was so glad that my mom had my hat. I am sure I would have lost it! You would love this roller coaster. I can't wait to ride it with you. See you soon!

Body often includes details and feelings about an interesting event

Other Closings
Sincerely
Your pal
Yours truly
Love
Best regards

Your friend,
Mario

Closing and Signature tell who wrote the letter

Thank-You Letter

In a **thank-you letter**, the author writes to a specific person to show appreciation for that person's words or actions.

Parts of a Thank-You Letter

- Heading, inside address, greeting, body, closing, and signature
- A body that clearly explains why the author is writing the letter
- Thoughts and feelings about the person or their actions
- A friendly voice that sounds like the author

Heading
Gives the sender's name date

Inside Address
The address of the person receiving the letter

Greeting
Addresses the person who the letter is written to

Body
Includes reasons for writing the letter and thoughts about the person or their actions

Closing and signature
Tell who wrote the letter

110 Fair Street
Tallahassee, FL 32301
December 15, 2012

Senator William Smith
100 North Adams Street
Tallahassee, FL 32301

Dear Senator Smith,

Thank you for visiting our school last week. I know you are very busy and it was nice of you to come talk to us. I learned a lot about government when you came to see us.

My favorite part of your talk was when you discussed voting. I know it is very important for us to vote. Being able to choose our government leaders is a great tradition in the United States. I wish I were old enough to vote now. Until then I will make sure my parents vote during each election.

Sincerely,
Adam Garcia
Third Grade

Other Closings
Regards
Thanks
Your friend
Yours truly

Personal Narrative

A **personal narrative** is a true story about an interesting or important event in the writer's life. A personal narrative about a writer's life may also be called an autobiography.

Parts of a Personal Narrative

- A beginning that pulls readers into the story
- Real events told in the order that they happened
- Interesting details about the people and events in the story
- A first-person point of view
- An ending that wraps up the story or tells how the writer felt

Beginning
Grabs the readers' attention

Middle
Tells what happened in time order

Interesting details describe sights, sounds, and feelings.

Learning to Fly

I will never forget the day I learned to fly. I didn't have wings, though, and I didn't use an airplane. All I had was a special jacket called a harness to keep me from falling to the ground. The activity is called zip-lining. I tried it for the first time when my family went on vacation to Montana.

At first I was scared to go zip-lining. My instructor, George, said that I would walk up a trail to a wooden deck. The deck was on the edge of a cliff 70 feet high! Then George would attach my harness to a long steel line. The line ran 200 feet across and ended at another deck below. Finally, I would jump off the top deck and zip through the air to the lower deck.

Walking up to the deck was the easy part. I liked looking up at all the tall trees

Other Transitions
First
Next
After that
During
After a while
Meanwhile
Later
Last

and hearing the birds sing. But as soon as we got to the deck, I became dizzy. My heart started to pound. I told George that I didn't think I could do it.

These paragraphs tell more about what happened and how the writer felt.

George patted me on the back and smiled. He said lots of people are scared at first. He explained how safe it was to go zip-lining. He said I looked very brave.

When I was ready, George attached my harness to the zip line. He reminded me to hold the rope that held my harness to the line. I took a deep breath and closed my eyes. Then I stepped off the deck.

Whoosh! The air whipped across my face and through my hair. I opened my eyes and saw the ground speed by below me. I was flying! George was right. Zip-lining was a lot of fun! It was even better than riding a roller coaster.

Ending
Tells how the story worked out and how the writer felt

My parents were waiting for me when I got to the lower deck. I gave them a big smile and a hug. Then I told them that I couldn't wait to go zip-lining again. After all, nothing is more exciting than flying!

Note how the author of this piece:

- Wrote an introduction that grabbed readers' attention.

- Other ways she could have introduced the story include asking the reader a question or jumping into the action.
  Have you ever watched a bird and wished you could fly?

  I gripped the rope on my harness and stared at the ground below.

Biography

A **biography** is a true story about a person's life. It tells why that person is special or interesting.

Parts of a Biography

- A beginning, middle, and end
- Interesting facts and details about the person
- Events told in time order

Theodor Seuss Geisel

Beginning
Gives the main idea or tells why the person is important

Theodor Seuss Geisel was born in 1904 in Springfield, Massachusetts. When Geisel was a boy, his mother often sang rhymes to him. He loved the rhymes. Geisel didn't know it then, but he would someday become famous for making rhymes of his own. People today know Theodor Geisel as Dr. Seuss. He wrote and illustrated more than 40 children's books.

Middle
Tells interesting facts and details about the person's life in time order

Theodor Geisel liked growing up in Springfield. His father worked in a city park with a zoo. Geisel spent a lot of time at the zoo. He liked to draw pictures of the animals he saw there. It's not surprising that many Dr. Seuss books have drawings of made-up animals.

Geisel left home in 1921. He went to college and then had a job drawing cartoons for many different magazines. He used the funny name Dr. Theophrastus Seuss for his drawings. Later, he shortened the name to Dr. Seuss.

Other Transitions
First
Next
After that
During
After a while
Meanwhile
Later
Last

In 1937, "Dr. Seuss" published his first children's book, *And to Think That I Saw It on Mulberry Street*. At first, publishers didn't like his book. Geisel had to send it to 27 different publishers before one of them accepted it! But readers loved Dr. Seuss's rhymes and cartoons. He published 10 more books between 1938 and 1956.

Geisel had a big challenge in 1957. His publisher asked him to write a book with only 225 different words. The words had to be ones that students in first grade could read on their own. Theodor wrote *The Cat in the Hat*. It became one of his most popular books. Three years later, he published *Green Eggs and Ham*. This book had only 50 different words.

End
Wraps up the biography and gives a final thought

Theodor Seuss Geisel died in 1991. His books have sold over 200 million copies. They also have been printed in 20 different languages. He was one of the world's greatest children's authors.

Note how the author of this piece:

- Wrapped up this piece by giving a final thought.

Other ways to conclude a biography include: explaining how the person's work is still being used today or telling how the person made a difference.

Theodor Geisel's books are still being read in homes and classrooms today.

Theodor Geisel made a difference in the lives of children around the world. He made reading fun.

Fictional Narrative

A **fictional narrative** is a made-up story. It tells about one or more characters who face a problem and shows how the problem is solved. The story is usually told in time order.

Parts of a Fictional Narrative

- A plot with a beginning, middle, and end
- A beginning that introduces the characters, setting, and problem
- Dialogue that shows what is happening or how the characters are feeling
- Strong action words and vivid descriptions
- An ending that shows how the problem is solved

Mystery at Midnight

Knock! Knock!

I pulled my bed covers up to my chin. What was that noise? I listened closely. Then I heard the strange sounds again. *Knock! Knock!*

"Jason!" I screamed. "Jason, come quick!"

My older brother opened my bedroom door.

"Geez, Mindy," he said. "I was asleep! Why are you yelling?"

"I hear strange noises."

"It's probably just the tree branches scraping your window." He yawned.

"No, it's inside my room." I sat up. "Listen."

Beginning
Introduces the characters, setting, and problem

Dialogue tells more about what is happening and how the characters are feeling.

Other Transitions
First
Next
After that
During
After a while
Meanwhile
Later
Last

Middle
Has rising action to make the story more exciting

Then I heard the noise again, but this time it wasn't a knock. It sounded like a butterfly was flapping its wings against my closet door. Jason tiptoed into my room. I jumped out of bed and stood next to him. "Did you hear that?" I asked.

"Yes," he whispered. "I think it's coming from in there." He pointed to my closet. Then he put his hand on the door knob. He slowly opened the closet door.

Strong action words and vivid descriptions create a clear picture for readers.

"Well, thank goodness!" a little voice said. "I've been trapped in there for hours!" Jason and I peeked into the closet. A small girl stood on one of my hangers. She was only six inches tall, and she had long, curly hair and two golden wings.

"Who are you?" I asked. "And why are you in my closet?"

"I'm the tooth fairy," she said with a smile. "I came to get your tooth, but I was a little early. I decided to hide in your closet until you went to sleep. Then you closed the door, and I got locked inside."

"Oops," I said. "Sorry about that!"

Ending
Tells how the story worked out or how the problem is solved

"It's okay," she said. "But now I'm late." She flew across the room and wiggled under my pillow. When she came out, she held my tooth in her hand. "Thanks for this," she said. "Your prize is under your pillow. Now how do I get out of here?"

Jason walked to my bedroom window and opened it. The little fairy flew to it, and then she stopped and winked. "See you next time!" she said. She flew away.

"Wow," Jason said. "That was crazy!" And we both began to laugh.

Play

A **play** is a story that is acted out in front of an audience. It uses dialogue, or what the characters say to each other, to tell a story.

✏ Parts of a Play

- A list of characters and a description of the setting
- Dialogue between two or more characters
- A beginning, middle, and end to the story
- Descriptions of what characters are doing

The Trial of Grumpy Gale

> A list gives a short description of each character.

CHARACTERS:
MOTHER NATURE: a kind, old lady
GRUMPY GALE: has wild hair; always frowning
VILLAGER: a farmer; late twenties

> The setting tells where or when the story takes place.

SETTING: The characters are seated in a court room. Mother Nature sits in the judge's chair behind a large desk. The villager and Grumpy Gale are seated in front of her.

MOTHER NATURE: (*in a gentle voice*) We are here today to hear complaints against Grumpy Gale, the strong wind of the north. Villager, you may begin.

> **Beginning**
> Tells what the story will be about or what the problem is

VILLAGER: (*stands and walks toward Mother Nature*) Mother Nature, the people of my village cannot stand Grumpy Gale for another day. He's just too grumpy! His strong winds never stop. He tears down our crops. He breaks the branches on our fruit trees. People are becoming hungry.

Details about what the characters are doing are put inside *parentheses*.

GRUMPY GALE: (*stands and speaks loudly*) I object! The people need to understand that I am very powerful. I must be strong to do my job well.

VILLAGER: But you are too strong! Mother Nature, please! Make Grumpy Gale take a vacation!

GRUMPY GALE: A vacation? Never!

MOTHER NATURE: Now, now, I'm sure I can come up with something to make you both happy. Gale, you used to be a gentle breeze. Do you remember that? You had so much fun making kites fly.

GRUMPY GALE: (*mumbling*) Yes, it was nice then. (*Loudly*) But I also like to be strong and powerful!

Middle
Develops the story and tells more about the problem

MOTHER NATURE: I think you can do both. In the fall and winter, you can be a strong and powerful wind. Then, in the spring and summer, you need to rest. You need to become a gentle breeze.

VILLAGER: That's a wonderful idea! The people in the village would be happy to have a gentle breeze.

MOTHER NATURE: Grumpy Gale, do you agree?

GRUMPY GALE: (*in a low, grumpy voice*) I guess so. It might be nice to fly a kite again.

End
Wraps up the story and tells how the problem is solved

MOTHER NATURE: Good, it's settled! Now, shake hands and go home. (*The villager and Grumpy Gale shake hands and leave the courtroom.*)

Poems

A **poem** is usually written in short lines and phrases. It has a rhythm, or beat, and it often uses rhyming words.

Parts of a Poem

- Exact words that create a clear picture for readers
- Onomatopoeia, or sound words, like *click* or *crash*
- Often, rhyming words at the ends of lines

pencils

> Rhyming words make a pattern of sounds

I giggled at the elephant.
I smiled at the clumsy giraffe.
A hippo slipped on a puddle.
His loud honking yell made me laugh.

> Onomatopoeia helps readers hear the sounds

When I turned to tell my sister,
SMACK! I walked right into a tree.
And as I rubbed my head, I heard
A mockingbird laughing at me!

Other Rhyming Words
Three, tree, bee
Tail, mail, trail
Wing, sing, thing
Fur, sure, purr
Bark, park, spark
Run, fun, done
Hair, bear, fair

> Exact words paint a clear picture

In black and white coats
The penguins stomp, spin, and clap.
I wish I could join their icy dance party.
Now the dancers break for lunch.
EW!
A bucket of slippery fish?
Then again, maybe I'll just visit the goats!

Clarabelle the cow had lots
of trouble with the barnyard dirt.
She swept her pasture every day,
and scrubbed her hooves until they hurt.

One day she mopped all the pig pens.
"Thanks!" oinked Max, who held the pail.
They watched the bucket tip and sway.
Splat! It soaked her, nose and tail.

A limerick is a special kind of poem.

Third grade is tough in Miss Jones's class.
She doesn't take any fooling or sass.
But she always is fair.
She helps us prepare
For tests so that we can all pass.

The fourth poem is a limerick, which is a five-line poem that has its own rhyme scheme.

Parts of a limerick:

- A first, second, and fifth line that rhyme

- A third and fourth line that rhyme

- Figurative language, such as onomatopoeia and similes

Opinion Essay

An **opinion essay** tells what a writer thinks about a topic. It also explains the reasons why the writer has this view.

✏️ Parts of an Opinion Essay

- An introduction that tells the writer's opinion and gives a focus statement
- Strong reasons that support the opinion
- Interesting, convincing details that explain the reasons
- A conclusion that sums up the opinion or repeats the focus statement

Introduction
Gives a focus statement with the writer's opinion

Reasons tell why the writer feels they way he or she does about a topic.

Details explain or support the reasons for the opinion.

The Best Pet

There are many different kinds of pets. Some people have a dog or a cat. They may even have a hamster. These animals are cute and fun, but they aren't the pets that I would choose. I think that a lizard makes the best pet.

First of all, lizards are fun to play with. My lizard, Al, sits on my shoulder while I do homework. He really likes it when I read to him. I also use blocks to build Al his own castle. Al sits inside the castle and scares people away. My friends love to play with Al when they come over. They pet his scaly skin and let him run across the floor.

Lizards are also easy to take care of. They don't need to be brushed or bathed. They don't even need to eat every day. I feed Al about three times a week. He eats

Other Transitions
First
Second
In addition
Next
As well as
For example
Later
Last

fruits, vegetables, and mealworms from the pet store. But the best part is that I don't have to worry about Al if I go away for the weekend. He's happy in his cage as long as it's clean and warm and there's water for him to drink.

Finally, it doesn't cost a lot to own a lizard. Lizards don't need toys or big bags of food. This can save you a lot of money at the pet store! And lizards don't need shots or special medicine. Al is three years old, but he's never had to go to the doctor. In fact, I can go for months without spending one penny on Al.

Conclusion Repeats the focus statement in a new way

Dogs, cats, and hamsters make good pets. But the greatest pet is a lizard. If you don't believe me, just ask Al.

Note how the author of this piece:

- Wrote a conclusion that re-stated the opinion in a new way.
  Other ways to end an essay include summing up the reasons for the opinion or giving a final thought.
  Lizards are fun, easy, and inexpensive.
  I have enjoyed owning a lizard more than any other pet.

- Used interesting details to explain the reasons for her opinion.
  My lizard, Al, sits on my shoulder while I do homework.

  I feed Al about three times a week. He eats fruits, vegetables, and mealworms from the pet store.

  Lizards don't need toys or big bags of food.

Persuasive Essay

A **persuasive essay** tries to convince readers to agree with a writer's opinion. The writer gives reasons to convince readers to take action or think a certain way.

Parts of a Persuasive Essay

- An introduction that tells the writer's opinion and goal
- Reasons that tell why readers should agree with the writer's opinion
- Details, facts, or examples that explain each reason
- A conclusion that sums up the writer's goal or reasons

Introduction Tells the writer's opinion and goal

School Garden

Our school made a lot of money at the spring carnival. Now the teachers and students have to decide how to spend it. Last night, I came up with a great idea. The money should be used to start a school garden.

First, a school garden will make recess better. Not all kids like playing tag and handball. Usually these kids just talk or read a book. But the garden

The writer gives strong reasons that readers will care about.

would give them something fun to do. They could water the plants. They could pick the ripe vegetables. They might even enjoy digging in the soil and pulling the weeds.

Second, a school garden will help students learn. The science teacher, Ms. Peabody, said she would use the school garden to teach about different

Other Transitions
To start with
Then
In addition
Next
As well as
For example
Later
Finally

kinds of plants. She also said that the garden would be a good place to do experiments. And that's not all! The health teacher could use the vegetables in the garden to teach students about healthy eating. The math teacher might even be able to use seeds from the garden to make counting and multiplication games. Students would have a great time learning in these ways.

Finally, a school garden could help raise money. The teachers and students could pick flowers and vegetables from the garden each week. Then they could sell them at the farmers' market. The money we make could pay for things like books and markers. It could also be used to buy more seeds and plants.

Building a school garden is the best way to spend the money that we made at the spring carnival. It will make recess better, help students learn, and raise even more money for the school. Everybody wins with a school garden!

Note how the author of this piece:

- Gave reasons that readers will care about.

Another way the writer could have connected with readers is by answering any questions or concerns they might have.

Some people think that we don't have the space for a school garden. But that's not true! The open field behind the basketball courts is the perfect place for a garden.

You might be wondering how long it will take to build the school garden. If everyone works together, we could do it in a week.

Response to a Play

A **response to a play** tells about a play that you've read or seen. It tells what the play is like and what you think about it.

✎ Parts of a Response to a Play

- An interesting introduction that mentions the title
- A focus statement that gives an opinion about a character or what happens in the play
- Details and examples from the play that support the opinion
- A conclusion that sums up the response

Introduction
Includes the title of the play and a focus statement

Monkey Tales

Have you ever felt like you don't fit in? Marvin the Monkey sure has! He is one of the characters in <u>Monkey Tales</u>. This funny and silly play shows just how different Marvin is from other monkeys.

To start, Marvin doesn't like bananas. He says that they feel mushy in his mouth. The other monkeys make fun of Marvin. They say he is a snob. This makes Marvin feel bad. But then he comes up with an idea. He makes crispy garlic bread and spaghetti. The other monkeys try his food and love it. They say, "Marvin may be different, but he sure is a good cook!"

Marvin is also scared to swing from trees. He's worried that he'll fall down. He says that swinging makes him sick. The other jungle animals try to teach Marvin how to swing, but it doesn't do any good.

Details and examples back up the writer's opinion and ideas.

Other Transitions
First
Second
Then
In addition
Next
So
As well as
Later
Finally

He wants to stick with running instead of swinging. Marvin even has a special pair of shoes that help him sprint around the jungle. This is one of the funniest parts in the play.

The last thing that makes Marvin so different is that he doesn't like sitting around all day like the other monkeys do. He wants to be a bus driver instead. He thinks it would be fun to drive around the jungle and meet new animals. Pepper Parrot tells Marvin that monkeys can't drive. But Marvin doesn't care. He says that everyone should have a dream.

Monkey Tales was the best play I have ever read! I loved how silly Marvin was. But the best thing about the play was that it showed that it's okay to be different. Maybe the play should get a new title: The Tale of the Misfit Monkey.

Conclusion Sums up the response and gives a final thought

Note how the author of this piece:

- Ordered his ideas in a way that makes sense. Good ways to organize a response essay include:
  - Moving from the least important idea to the most important
  - Moving from the most important idea to the least important
  - Giving examples from the selection in time order

- Used connecting words to link the paragraphs.

To start, Marvin doesn't like bananas.
Marvin is also scared to swing from trees.
The last thing that makes Marvin so different is that he doesn't like sitting around all day like the other monkeys do.

Response to Poetry

A **response to poetry** discusses a poem that you've read and tells what you think about it.

✎ Parts of a Response to Poetry

- An interesting introduction that mentions the title of the poem
- A focus statement that gives an opinion about the poem
- Details and examples from the poem that support the opinion
- A conclusion that sums up the response

A poem →

Mary Had a Lazy Lamb

Mary has a lazy lamb,
He won't get out of bed,
And every time that Mary tries,
He bleats and shakes his head.

She tugs on his collar,
She bangs pots and pans,
On his head, she pours water,
Then she claps her hands.

Mary gets very mad,
She shouts and she moans,
Then the lamb gets up,
With great yawns and groans.

He wants to eat grass,
And stay on the front lawn,

Mary has to go to school,
But there's grass to munch on.

"The walk is too long!"
The lazy lamb cries,
Mary tugs on his leash,
She pulls and she sighs.

She is late for school,
She misses a test,
The lazy lamb naps,
"I need plenty of rest!"

"Make all the children laugh and play,
My friends are very shy!"
The lamb ignores Mary's pleas,
And makes a young boy cry.

The lamb sleeps on a girl's lunch,
And ruins all the food,
So Mary shares her sandwich,
And everything tastes good.

But now Mary is hungry,
Her stomach growls all day,
Soon the school day ends,
But now the sky is gray.

Mary pulls the lamb's leash,
She feels like a great fool,
"That's it!" she cries, "Never again,
Will I bring my lazy lamb to school!"

continued

Mary Had a Lazy Lamb

If you've ever had a bad day, you will love the poem "Mary Had a Lazy Lamb." The poem tells about Mary's very bad day. And it's all because of her lazy lamb.

First, Mary's lamb won't get out of bed in the morning. Mary pulls on his collar. She bangs pots and pans. She pours water on his face. Mary gets very mad. The lamb finally gets up, but he groans a lot. I thought this would make Mary's day better. But her problems are just beginning.

Next, Mary's lamb won't follow her to school. He wants to stay in Mary's front yard and eat grass instead. He says that the walk is too long. Mary has to put a leash on the lamb and drag him to school. This makes Mary so late for school that she misses a test. I felt very bad for Mary!

Then Mary's lazy lamb causes more trouble. Mary says her friends are shy. She wants the lamb to make them laugh and

Other Transitions
To start with
Second
Then
In addition
Next
So
As well as
Later
Last

play. But the lamb does something very different. He makes a boy cry! Then the lamb takes a nap on someone's lunch. The lunch is ruined, so Mary shares her sandwich. This leaves Mary feeling hungry. The poem says that, "her stomach growls all day."

Finally, Mary's lamb won't walk home after school. Mary feels very foolish. She says, "That's it! Never again will I bring my lazy lamb to school."

The writer shares thoughts and feelings about the poem.

I think that "Mary Had a Lazy Lamb" is a very funny poem. I could tell Mary got very mad at her lamb. That lamb was a lot of trouble!

Conclusion Sums up the response and gives a final thought

I'm sure you will enjoy this poem, too. Mary had a rough day with her lazy lamb. I felt bad for her, but I laughed, too. The poem sure makes me feel that my bad days aren't so bad after all.

Note how the author of this piece:

- Ordered her ideas in a way that makes sense. Good ways to organize a response essay include:
  - Moving from the least important idea to the most important
  - Moving from the most important idea to the least important
  - Giving examples from the selection in time order

- Used a strong transition at the beginning of each paragraph.

  First, Mary's lamb won't get out of bed in the morning.

  Next, Mary's lamb won't follow her to school.

  Finally, Mary's lamb won't walk home after school.

Author Response

An **author response** compares two stories or books written by the same author.

Parts of an Author Response Essay

- An introduction to the main characters
- A brief review of the plot for each story
- A review of the similarities and differences in the two stories

pencils

Stuart Little and Charlotte's Web

Introduction
Introduces the books and the author

Two books I have enjoyed are *Stuart Little* and *Charlotte's Web*. Both books were written by E.B. White and are considered classics today.

Body
Reviews the plot of each book and describes their similarities and differences

Both books tell very different stories. *Stuart Little* is about a mouse named Stuart. He is raised by a family of humans and has a lot of fun adventures. Stuart has a good friend Margalo, who is a bird. On the other hand, *Charlotte's Web* is about a pig named Wilbur and his friend Charlotte, who is a spider. Wilbur seems like an ordinary pig, but with the help of Charlotte, he becomes really famous.

Here, the author summarizes how the books are similar.

One way the books are similar is that both books are about friendship. The main characters in each book grow up in strange places and don't really fit in. They both get lonely, too. The thing that helps both Stuart and Wilbur through hard times is finding a good friend. Margalo saved Stuart's life a couple of times. Meanwhile, Charlotte saved Wilbur's

Other Transitions
At first
Anyway
Even though
After that
Eventually
Soon
Finally
Near the end

In this paragraph, the author examines how the two books are different.

life many times and taught him that everyone is special, even a pig.

Stuart Little and Charlotte's Web have many things in common. But they also have several things that are quite different. One way they are different is the way each book ends. In Stuart Little, the book ends by Stuart going to look for his good friend Margalo. The story doesn't feel finished, and the reader has to imagine what might happen next. On the other hand, Charlotte's Web has a great ending. Though Wilbur was sad when Charlotte died, everything worked out in the end. Charlotte had little baby spiders that stayed with Wilbur and became his friends.

Both books are very well-written. E.B. White is a great author. His characters are very lifelike, and there is a lot of emotion in his writing. I got really sad when Charlotte died at the end of Charlotte's Web. This is a good sign of a great writer. E.B. White is good at describing feelings.

Conclusion Summarizes the books and gives an opinion about them

Stuart Little and Charlotte's Web are classic novels for kids. All kids should read these novels because they are great stories about friendship. Through these books, E.B. White tells us that everyone is special. Even a pig and a little mouse can teach us how to be nice to each other.

Note how the author of this piece:

- Puts the title of each book in *italics*.

- Tells about what makes the author's books special.

  His characters are very life-like and there is a lot of emotion in his writing.

Book Review

A **book review** tells the reader about a book. This type of essay tells about the characters and plot, and the author gives an opinion about the book.

Parts of a Book Review

- An introduction that describes the name of the book and its author
- A body that details the characters, main conflict, and plot
- A conclusion that reviews the main points and explains the author's opinion

Introduction
Tells the title of the book and who wrote it

Body
Explains the book's main characters and plot

Charlotte's Web

The book *Charlotte's Web* by E.B. White is about a pig named Wilbur and his friend Charlotte, who is a spider. It is a great story about friendship.

Most of the book takes place on a farm. A girl named Fern raises Wilbur and takes care of him. Wilbur is a runt and very small for a pig. One day Wilbur is sold to a farm nearby. Fern goes to visit him as often as she can. After some time, Fern can't see Wilbur much, and he starts to get lonely.

One day, while in the barn, Wilbur meets a spider named Charlotte. Charlotte is very smart and full of good advice. Soon Wilbur and Charlotte become very good friends. Wilbur meets a lot of other farm animals, too, including a funny rat named Templeton. Templeton seems pretty selfish, but he has a good heart.

Other Transitions
After some time
One day
Soon
One night
By this time
Before

The conflict is the main problem that needs to be solved by the characters.

This paragraph describes how the characters solved the problem.

This paragraph describes how the story ended.

Conclusion Reviews the main points of the book and explains why the author liked or disliked the book

One night one of the old sheep tells Wilbur the farmer plans to eat him for Christmas dinner. Wilbur and his friends get very worried. Charlotte then gets an idea to write words in her web about Wilbur. She thinks this idea might save Wilbur.

Templeton helps by getting pieces of newspaper with words on them and gives them to Charlotte. These words are adjectives that describe Wilbur. Charlotte spells out things like "some pig" and "terrific." The farmer notices the words and decides not to eat Wilbur. Instead he brings Wilbur to the county fair. At the fair, Wilbur wins a prize and becomes famous.

By this time Charlotte is really old for a spider. She dies while at the fair with Wilbur. Wilbur is very sad about losing his best friend. Before she died, though, Charlotte left behind a sac of eggs. Wilbur brings the egg sac back to the farm with him. Soon the eggs hatch. Most of the baby spiders leave the farm but three stay behind. They soon become Wilbur's new friends at the farm.

Charlotte's Web is a wonderful book. It is a great story about friendship. I liked a lot of the characters in the book, especially the rat Templeton. My favorite part of the book was all the talking animals. It was very sad when Charlotte died, and I felt bad for Wilbur. But everything worked out in the end, and Wilbur got new friends. E.B. White is a really good writer. This is a great book, and I would tell other people to read it.

Persuasive Speech

A **persuasive speech** tries to convince an audience about something. The author uses facts to argue his or her opinion about a subject.

Parts of a Persuasive Speech

- An introduction that describes the main arguments
- Supporting arguments backed up with details or facts
- A conclusion that restates the main argument and supporting ideas

Introduction
Tells the subject and the author's main arguments

Body
Gives details and facts that support the author's arguments

Each body paragraph gives details about one topic.

Why We Should Get a Cat

I think that getting a cat is a great idea. Cats are very easy to take care of. They are also fun to have around the house. Owning a cat would teach me how to be more responsible. There are so many reasons why we should get a cat.

First, cats are not hard to take care of. Unlike some animals, cats only need food twice a day. Dogs eat lots of dog food and human food. They will eat anything they can get their paws on! On the other hand, cats only eat about a half a cup of cat food a day. That will save money and time. Cats also save time because they take care of themselves. They lick themselves to stay clean, so you will not have to give them a bath. They also don't need to be taken for a walk. Cats can do so much on their own!

Second, cats are lots of fun. They like to play with toys. You don't even need to

Other Transitions
Although
Sometimes
After that
Once in a while
Even though
Meanwhile
Lastly
In closing

spend much money to keep them busy. A simple piece of yarn will make a cat run, leap, and roll. Although they have a lot of energy, they also like to relax. A cat is like a cuddly blanket. When it is chilly outside, a cat will keep you warm by sitting on your lap.

Finally, a good reason to get a cat is that I could learn about responsibility. You might be wondering who will take care of the cat. Even though cats do not take much time, parents are still very busy and might not have time for a pet. However, you don't have to worry. I would be the person who takes care of the cat. I would feed the cat twice a day. I would also change the kitty litter. Having a cat would teach me how to take care of things.

Conclusion Reviews the writer's opinions and makes a final statement

There are so many reasons why we should get a cat. What other pet is so easy and fun? I know you agree that a cat will be a perfect pet for our family. Let's go pick one out today!

Note how the author of this piece:

- Answers a question that her audience might have.

  You might be wondering who will take care of the cat...
  I would be the person who takes care of the cat.

- Ends her speech with an encouraging statement.

  Other ways she could have ended her speech are to give a fact or a quote.

  Scientists say that people with cats often live longer because cats are so relaxing.

  As Charles Dickens said, "What greater gift than the love of a cat?"

Labels and Captions

A **label** tells what a picture is or shows the parts of something. A **caption** adds information to a picture or explains an idea. A label uses one or a few words. A caption includes one or more complete sentences.

pencils

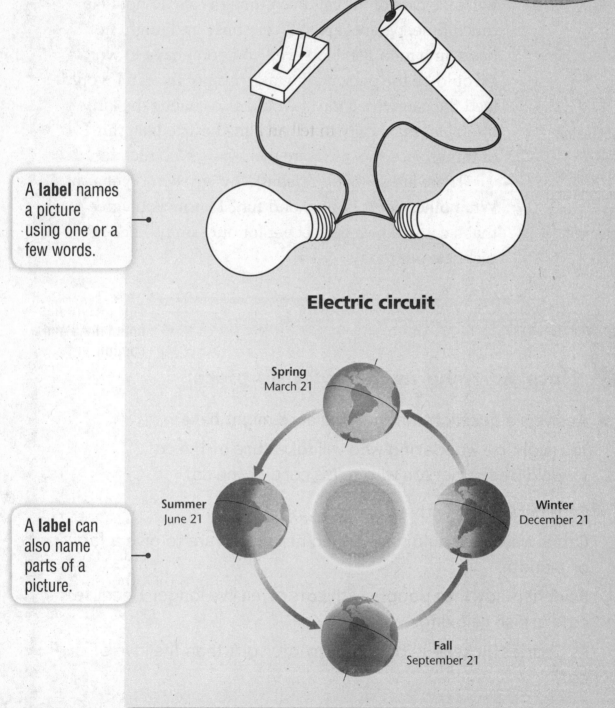

A **label** names a picture using one or a few words.

Electric circuit

A **label** can also name parts of a picture.

Spring
March 21

Summer
June 21

Winter
December 21

Fall
September 21

A **caption** uses complete sentences to add information to a picture.

The easiest way to tell an alligator from a crocodile is to compare their snouts. A crocodile has a long, narrow, V-shaped snout. An alligator's snout is wider and U-Shaped.

This picture has both labels and a caption.

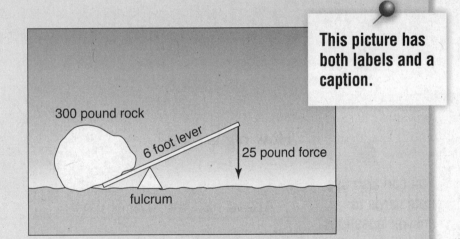

300 pound rock

6 foot lever

25 pound force

fulcrum

A **caption** can also explain an idea—how something works or what it does.

A lever works by pushing down on one side of the fulcrum. This causes the load on the other side of the fulcrum to lift up.

Notetaking Strategies

Notetaking helps you to remember important information. You can take notes while reading, listening, or watching a demonstration or video.

Note cards help you take notes while reading. Each card has:
One main idea
Facts and details
The source where you found the information

Mars

—atmosphere mostly carbon dioxide

—iron in soil makes it look red

—poles are covered in ice.

—orbits the sun every 637 days

Source: <u>Amazing Mars</u> p.23

Main idea

Facts and details

The source

You can also use note cards to answer questions.

How big is Mars?

About half the size of earth

Diameter 4,222 miles

Source: <u>Amazing Mars</u> p.7

Write the question you want to answer on the first line.

Write the answer.

Tell where you found the answer.

Story charts can help you take notes while reading fiction books. A story chart is a good way to take notes for a book report or summary.

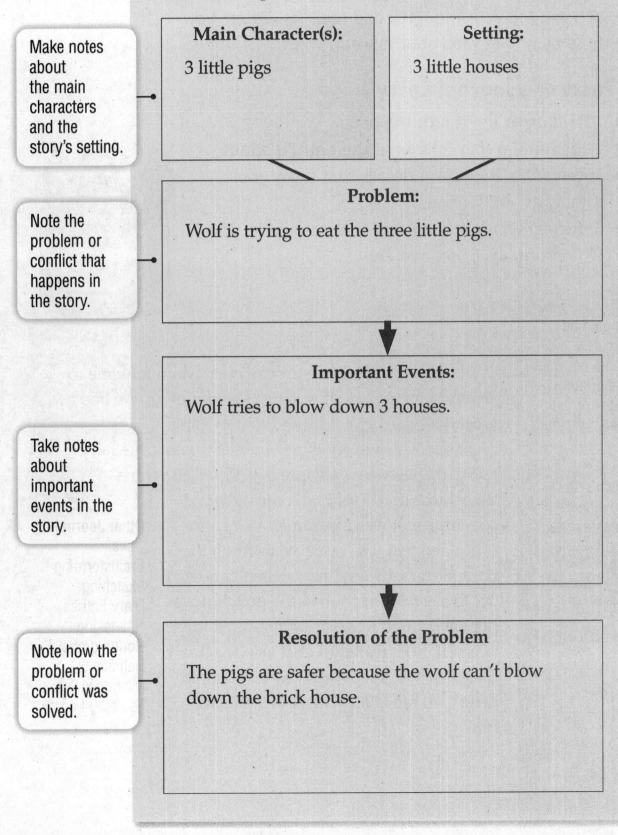

Make notes about the main characters and the story's setting.

Main Character(s):

3 little pigs

Setting:

3 little houses

Note the problem or conflict that happens in the story.

Problem:

Wolf is trying to eat the three little pigs.

Take notes about important events in the story.

Important Events:

Wolf tries to blow down 3 houses.

Note how the problem or conflict was solved.

Resolution of the Problem

The pigs are safer because the wolf can't blow down the brick house.

Journal

A **journal** is a notebook in which you can write about anything you want. You can tell a true story about your life. You can tell your thoughts and feelings. Often, you are the only one to read your journal.

Parts of a Journal Entry

- The date at the top of the page
- A beginning that tells what the entry is about
- Interesting, important details that show your thoughts and feelings
- Informal words and phrases that sound like you
- The pronouns *I*, *me*, and *we*

Beginning
Perhaps tells about an important event or main idea

Details show why the event was important and how you felt.

March 24

Today I got the best surprise ever! Mom took me to an amusement park. It was just the two of us. We had a great day!

As soon as we got there, we met my favorite fairy tale hero. She was really pretty and talked with a funny accent. She told us some of her adventures. It was awesome!

When that was over, we went on the bumper cars. I was super excited because I got to steer. Mom pushed the pedals. I was not tall enough to reach. Mom called me "Peanut"! I'm really good at steering, but I made Mom think I wasn't so that I could drive into the other cars. It was a lot of fun!

Other Journal Uses
Brainstorming
Sketching
Diary Entries
Notetaking
Rough drafts
Definitions
Memories
Learning Log

Pronouns *I*, *me*, and *we* show that it is about you or someone else.

After that we went on the spinning tea cups. We went pretty fast. It was fun! Afterward, I was so dizzy I could hardly walk.

I was not too dizzy for a snack, though! We got chocolate space ice cream. That was really cool. It's not like normal ice cream. It looks like rocks or pebbles, but it tastes really good.

I wanted to go on the roller coasters, but I'm still too short for those. Mom says maybe next year I'll be tall enough. The roller coasters look really fun! Mom doesn't like roller coasters because she is afraid of heights. But I can't wait until I'm tall enough!

It was great to spend time with Mom and to try all these fun rides. Maybe next time we'll bring Dad and Joey. I'd like to take my friend Samantha, too.

It was a really great day! I hope we go back many times this summer.

Ending
Wraps up the journal entry

Note how the author of this piece:

- Wrote about something that happened to her.

She also could have used her journal to write about something she learned in school.

Today we studied Helen Keller in history class. I think she was a really interesting person.

- Included plenty of details about what happened.

She was really pretty and talked with a funny accent.
It looks like rocks or pebbles, but it tastes really good.

Index